John Greechan is an Edinburgh-based sports writer and communications consultant. During 30 years in Scotland and England, including almost two decades as Chief Sports Writer with the *Scottish Daily Mail*, his remit has ranged from non-league assignments to coverage of the Olympics, the rugby World Cup and golf's Open Championship. His most recent work has earned a place on the shortlist for the Columnist of the Year and Interviewer of the Year in the 2023 Scottish Press Awards. John's love of sport extends to a passion for coaching and tactics – he holds a UEFA C Licence and an SFA Talent ID Award as well as the Certificate in Advanced Football Tactical Analysis from the Barca Innovation Hub Universitas.

REVOLUTION
Ange Postecoglou

The man, the methods and the mastery

JOHN GREECHAN

For Dad, who took his young family to Canada in that wave of 1970s emigration, worked the night shift, day shift, back shift and every other hour available – but was never too tired to talk about football. And Mum, always on hand to remind us that trying your best and having fun was more important than winning or losing. Oh and, of course, Lucas. Who knows more about the game than I ever will.

This edition first published in 2024 by
Arena Sport, an imprint of
Birlinn Limited
West Newington House
10 Newington Road
Edinburgh
EH9 1QS

www.birlinn.co.uk

ISBN 978 1 913759 20 9

British Library Cataloguing-in-Publication Data
A catalogue record for this book is available from the British Library

Typeset by Hewer Text (UK) Ltd, Edinburgh

Papers used by Birlinn are from well-managed forests and other responsible sources

Printed and bound by Clays Ltd, Elcograf S.p.A.

CONTENTS

ACKNOWLEDGEMENTS

I have to start by acknowledging the many friends and former colleagues of Ange who were so generous with their time and insight. The six days I spent in Melbourne, speaking to those who worked with Postecoglou and kicking around his old neighbourhood of Prahran, was an absolute blast. I arrived with one appointment in the diary and left with enough material to fill two books. Everyone I spoke to was of great help – but special mention must go to Stevie Blair for the brilliant photos and plentiful laughs.

It would also be remiss of me not to thank my better half, Rhona, for being the first to read every chapter. Her feedback and advice were invaluable.

And then there are the folks at Birlinn, starting with Paul Smith for approaching me with the perfect project and guiding this newbie through the process, but also including copy-editor Ian Greensill and the countless other unsung heroes who turn an idea into an actual book. Top work, folks. Take the rest of the afternoon off.

Introduction

FROM SOUTH MELBOURNE TO NORTH LONDON

WHAT a journey it's been. What an adventure for the little Greek boy who spent many a late Melbourne night watching grainy TV broadcasts of English football, sharing special bonding moments with his steadfastly pragmatic father, a hard man who would soften while drawing his son's attention to the artists dancing around the assassins during an era of blood, thunder, grace and beauty. Ange Postecoglou's rise to the job of Tottenham Hotspur manager may not be the most improbable of developments in a game hardly short of epic ascents. In terms of sheer distance covered and weight divisions conquered, however, the kid from Prahran – a suburb still heavily influenced by one of the most impactful immigrant groups in global history – has certainly come a very long way. On a path that, in retrospect, was always destined to include a stop at one of England's most famous clubs. Greek by birth, Australian by choice and a citizen of the world when it comes to football, there is no denying the influence the English game has played upon his development.

Steered towards the swashbuckling Leeds side of the 1970s by the firm hand of dad, Jim, a young Ange fell head over heels for Liverpool – Kenny Dalglish remains his sporting idol – as he immersed himself in the one league guaranteed to find coverage in Australia, with its plethora of ten-pound Poms and strong links with the UK. It would be impossible to overstate how important the English game was, not just to Anglo ex-pats but to all European immigrants eager for a footballing fix in the land of unfamiliar codes and dismissive attitudes, during those formative years for Postecoglou. There's an entire generation of 'new Australians' who grew up learning about football from Hugh Johns – best known here for his long stints in many a Midlands commentary booth – on ITV's *Star Soccer* programme which, along with *Match of the Day* and, later, *The Big Match*, provided a heavily anglicised sporting diet for anyone seeking a break from Aussie Rules, cricket and, in some areas, rugby (league or union). And, while the local Greek-language newspaper might have been the source of all wisdom about a South Melbourne Hellas team yet to have its 'ethnic' name stripped from the records, Postecoglou used to read and re-read the same *Shoot!* and *Match* magazines so popular with youngsters back in the UK. He just had to wait a month for the latest edition to appear in the one book shop – and there was only one – guaranteed to stock even an outdated English publication.

So, absolutely, his admiration for the great Dutch Total Voetbal teams of Johan Cruyff et al. became an overriding influence on how he wanted his own sides to play. Yet he also developed a special regard for teams who could pass and move with similar precision – and do it amid the maelstrom of a game where pace and power were still such an enormous factor. The old First Division had an authenticity that hooked him and his pals from the off.

This fascination was only strengthened when Arsenal Double winner and all-round fashion icon Charlie George made a couple of guest appearances for South. The buzz a young Ange got from watching former Newcastle, Arsenal and England striker Malcolm 'Supermac' Macdonald run through defenders in his three National Soccer League appearances for Hellas left him with an abiding respect, not always noticed amid the pretty patterns of play, for a proper centre forward capable of bullying opponents.

It is, of course, fair to say that the arrival of Ange in North London left some Spurs supporters dumbfounded and others, quite frankly, apoplectic that their perpetually crisis-stricken club were appointing some complete nobody who had – TRIGGER WARNING FOR CELTIC FANS – 'only ever done it in Scotland . . .' For those who knew the full Postecoglou story, however, there was optimism that he'd make an impact.

And, in so many ways, it made sense that he'd be given a chance in the world's most exciting (trademark pending) league at this late stage of a nomadic career. There's a feeling that his footballing odyssey wouldn't have been complete without a chance to coach in England. If, like those old editions of *Shoot!* and *Match*, he's taken a little longer to reach his destination, well, you have to consider the sheer mileage racked up during his 59 years on earth. And take account of where it all began.

Chapter 1

HIS FATHER'S SON, HIS OWN MAN

THERE are many remarkable aspects to Ange Postecoglou's personal journey through time and space. There is also a universality to his story that should appeal to an audience far beyond football. Anyone who ever loved their dad, for instance. Or felt excluded from society, for whatever reason. All who know how it feels to sacrifice little bits of their soul in order to pursue something more important than personal joy or satisfaction, of course. And those who understand that, as important as sport is to hundreds of millions around the globe, games for games' sake will never be enough. All should find signs of a kindred spirit, or similarities with episodes from their own lives, in this story of single-minded application to the pursuit of success. Or, rather, success with style.

Because to paint the Tottenham manager as some one-note obsessive, to describe him only in terms of someone who has given too many hours and too many cares to building a career through selfless dedication to training plans, tactical ploys and the difficult art of man management, would be entirely unfair. He's so much more interesting than that. And, to hear those who have worked for, lost arguments with – and occasionally even provoked a smile from – Ange over the years, he's always been something of an oddity. In the very best way.

If we are all products of our environment, at least to some degree, then it is little wonder that Postecoglou has developed such a cosmopolitan outlook on football and, almost as importantly, life. Because immigrant kids like him have to be trailblazers. It's not an optional extra. Dragged halfway across the world by parents who want only a better life for their offspring, it's the youngsters who become experts in the art of integrating into new surroundings. They have no choice but to find a middle ground, holding on – often subconsciously – to the best elements of their own family culture while always striving to prove that they belong in their new country. Ange is a case in point.

He's no longer the little Greek boy who led his school's first soccer team – wearing hand-me-down sleeveless Aussie Rules jerseys and shorts tight enough to cause a delay in the voice-breaking process – to a state championship, as player-coach, at the age of 12. But the work ethic instilled in him, as a member of an expat community grafting to improve their lot in Melbourne, remains unaltered. The understanding that effort is the most important element of any job has stuck with him.

That is, of course, a common trait among children whose parents up sticks on a journey from the old world to the new. As a Greek-born citizen of the world who landed in Australia at the age of five, Postecoglou was immediately immersed in a community with an insatiable desire to prove a point. Or six. Or ten. Whatever it took. For as long as it takes.

That's another thing you need to know about him. He's self-aware enough to recognise that no number of summits breached will ever be enough. Not for someone whose ambitions go far beyond merely winning and losing. This is a rare quality in a football coach, many of whom are constantly trying to convince themselves that one more trophy or one last big job will bring lasting contentment. Postecoglou is highly unlikely to be found indulging in such delusional dancing around the hard truth. With him, talk is more likely to focus on legacy than achievement. He's a lifer. Has been since his unquestioning mates simply accepted that he'd be the gaffer of their Year 7 team at Prahran High School.

No one should underestimate the sheer gall it took for him and his pals to press ahead with establishing the school's first team in a sport mocked and scorned by their fellow pupils. Not just because the teacher assigned to coach them was happy to let that pushy Postecoglou lad take on the burden of leadership. Most would probably recognise that as a very fortunate twist of fate, for all concerned.

But merely the act of sticking with football, very much an 'ethnic' sport in a part of Australia where footy meant something extremely different, indeed, said something about a young Ange's refusal to be cowed. Life in the colonies, in the 1970s, wasn't always easy for anyone who didn't conform to the new realities emerging as the last vestiges of Empire were shaken loose. As they sought to establish themselves as more than merely dominions of the UK, countries like Australia and Canada clung to their own home-grown sports as methods of self-expression. It was very easy for kids to feel like second-class citizens because their parents spoke a different language, or at least with a very different accent, and retained an interest in 'foreign' games. The peer pressure to fit in, to take up AFL in Victoria or ice hockey in Ontario, could be overwhelming. Kudos to Ange, then, for taking the more difficult path.

If he was doing it just for himself, of course, it would never have worked. If he'd been motivated purely by a love of the game and the enjoyment that comes with playing well, there is no way he would have endured or reached such heights. Since that first game as a manager, he's needed a better reason – a cause, if you like – to make the challenge worthwhile. Because it has taken an enormous amount of discipline to get this far. Not just the long days and nights spent poring over Xs and Os on a tactics board or reading any coaching book he could access. But the intentional cutting of ties – the conscious decision to remain as aloof from his players as the voice of God delivering commandments that shall be obeyed, without ever losing the human touch that makes management more of an alchemy than a pure science – has to have taken its toll. Yet here he stands. Content. Or as content as any competitor can be. A totemic figure for more than one people.

Representation matters? Well, he's representing just about everyone. The entire Greek community who gravitated towards South Melbourne Hellas FC almost from the moment they passed through immigration, knowing that they'd be landing in a place where the people could, first of all, understand what they were saying. Ever since the earliest days of massed economic migration, football clubs have provided as much of a focal point, a place to find a job, maybe even meet a spouse, if the gods were shining on you, as any non-secular house of worship or well-meaning community group. Hellas was a case in point for Jim Postecoglou, who arrived by boat – in itself something of a throwback, in a new age of jet travel – alongside wife Voula, ten-year-old daughter Elizabeth and young Angelos in 1970. Forced out of Greece by a government drive towards nationalising businesses, his own furniture-making firm included, Jim loved match day for reasons that went beyond the quality of the game. So, yes, ask the Maikousis, Galatas, Deligiannis or Filopoulos clans now thriving in Victoria about Ange and they'll waste no time in claiming him as one of their own. It's not even up for debate, mate.

If the average Aussie sports fan might have been slower to embrace a man who went on to become a successful Socceroos boss, by anyone's measure, there's no denying that the folks Down Under also see Ange as a home-grown success story. After all, he played his entire career in a domestic setting, then led South Melbourne – shorn of the Hellas tag by now – to the inaugural FIFA World Club Championship as manager. He's taken their bold sense of adventure, the idea of showing the world what Australian get-up-and-go can achieve, and melded it into his character. If he will always enjoy a complicated relationship with his adopted homeland, with his constant striving to improve football in Oz meaning he is forever pointing out flaws in the way things are done, everything he achieved in Scotland – and whatever he achieves in England – reflects on Soccer Australia.

The Japanese also see him as an ambassador for the game, courtesy of both his time in the J.League and the lessons he continues to draw on from his time there. He's not just someone who raids their clubs for players, an irksome sign of approval in itself, but a coach whose own success in European football underlines the idea that Japan – the country, its culture and its approach to football – has something valuable to contribute to the beautiful game. The lessons he learned with Yokohama F. Marinos were evident in the way Celtic played for two beautiful seasons. The experience changed him. And it is yet another prime example of how he has benefited from scouring the world for players, for insight and for lessons that might help him to become a better coach.

But it can all be traced back to Albert Park, home to both the new and old South Melbourne FC grounds, and the neighbouring suburb of Prahran. Just as Sir Alex Ferguson will always credit Harmony Row Boys' Club in Glasgow for the grounding he received, so Ange will forever be linked with the place where it all started.

In this book, you'll read a few choice words from the man himself, because some of his most profound and interesting statements – either recorded for posterity in mile-high headlines or partially buried under the day's news agenda – bear repeating. Renowned for his motivational speeches, his opinions on the game are always worth examining.

But the bulk of the work here has come from long discussions with old friends and team-mates, much of it drawn from a thoroughly enjoyable trip to Melbourne, travelling to sit down with the people who played alongside him, worked under him as a coach – or even played a part in handing him his first managerial job. Very few requests for time were ignored or allowed to drift. None prompted a flat-out refusal. And those who spoke all shared an almost evangelical zeal for the subject. Like long-time disciples who have always recognised 'The Truth', they're delighted that the gospel according to Ange is being spread more widely and winning armies of new converts.

There is nothing po-faced about his legion of old friends and admirers, however. A great proportion of time spent researching this book involved laughing like a drain at something ridiculous – a frog infestation on the field where one of the most important games in Postecoglou's managerial career took place, for instance – or simply silly, such as old team-mate Steve Blair's photo of a younger (and skinnier) Ange squeezing himself into a turnstile at Celtic Park, back when no one could have imagined that this guy – a part-time footballer who worked in a bank while playing for Australia's leading club – would one day return as manager.

Tales of his time working under Hungarian legend Ferenc Puskás, using their shared knowledge of Greek to constantly pick the brains of the Galloping Major himself, point to a constant desire to capitalise on every opportunity and gather up as much information as possible. Use every tool at his disposal to improve as a player and then as a coach. At heart, he's still the same kid who used to take the tram into central Melbourne to devour every football magazine and book available at the one shop where 'soccer' fans could find what they needed. And, oh, he needed it. Craved it.

Lifelong friend Nick Deligiannis, who has known Postecoglou for nigh on half a century, took up the story as he recalled: 'I actually met Ange the first day of football, when we went down to South Melbourne, whom he ended up captaining and coaching to all those championships. We were eight or nine. And we've literally been best mates since then, so we go back a long way.

'We were aspiring young fellas going to the biggest club in town. It was definitely the biggest Greek club so, being from a Greek background, as most of the kids were back then, it was *the* big club. It went on to become really successful, obviously, but it was always one of the big clubs in Australia. We were all aspiring players. I ended up playing for Heidelberg, a competitor team in the national league, while Ange stayed and went through the ranks, captaining and coaching, all of that.

'Even early doors, on the first day I met him, he was an organiser. He was eight years old and was trying to organise stuff. He was a determined little bugger, as well! So I remember thinking he had a bit about him. We've been mates ever since.'

Deligiannis now works in recruitment, rising to become managing director of one of Australia's leading firms in that field, which means he's spent a professional lifetime in the business of identifying talent. He spotted the potential in his best mate pretty early, marvelling at the chutzpah it took to set up that school team and pointing out: 'Unless Ange stepped up, they wouldn't have had anything.'

The fact that Prahran would go on to win the State Championship, with the final played at Hellas' home ground, earned the immigrant kids some well-deserved admiration from those who already loved the game – and a bit of grudging acknowledgement from the Aussies. That hardly seems a fitting reward for Ange planning training, organising tactics and spending eight cents of his 20 cents lunch money to buy the *Herald Sun*, purely for the sports section. Yeah, he was that kid, the one who walked around school with a newspaper under his arm. The boy who pored over every frame in a three-month-old *Roy of the Rovers* comic imported from the UK.

Even back then, though, he wasn't doing it for praise. In a country that likes to pride itself on everyone getting a 'fair go', he was trying to prove that he and his friends were at least equal to the all-Australian kids boasting a couple of generations' head start. Postecoglou has often spoken about the need to have motivation beyond titles and silverware, insisting that 'the pursuit of winning and trophies without attaching any meaning to what you're doing is like chasing the wind.' That started in Prahran. It started with a need to prove himself.

This was, after all, a child who – at the age of just ten – began to dream about coaching at a World Cup. Not playing. Coaching. An admirable ambition. For the longest time, however, it must have seemed about as realistic as becoming the first man to run a three-minute mile. What on earth made him think that could ever happen?

In many ways, his journey has echoes with the similarly stratospheric strides taken by someone like Commander Chris Hadfield, possibly the most famous spaceman of the 21st century. When former International Space Station commander Hadfield was a kid dreaming of going to the stars, there was literally no such thing as a Canadian astronaut. It was an impossibility. Barred by an act of US Congress, effectively. But it didn't stop him. For a little Greek-Australian boy growing up in a country where there was no full-time professional football, harbouring an ambition to coach on the global stage – a goal he would achieve with the Socceroos in 2014 – must have seemed as distant as the furthest star in the sky. There's something faintly ridiculous about the ability of certain people to bend the world to their will.

'Just from having known him for such a long period of time, he's obviously very determined and very focused,' said Deligiannis. 'He's also very competitive and wants to do well. But it's more than just winning. Winning is clearly super important but, to him, it's about doing it the right way, the way he believes in, philosophically. He's got that really strong sense of doing things the right way in order to build something that will be a legacy, a way that football – in his eyes – needs to be played. So it's not just about success. It's about playing football that is attractive and football that allows you to control a game. You can win without control but he wouldn't want that.

'Everything he does is aligned to that philosophy. And I've seen this a lot now, how much he values loyalty to the idea. If you're aligned to that philosophy, you are exactly what he wants, looks for and needs. Conversely, and he never does it rudely or anything, if you're not that, it's just a fact that you won't hang around. Because he needs to have people who will do things the way he wants it. He's very determined about that.

'And he's a very smart guy, a very intelligent guy. The thing that separated him here – and I'm not commenting on anyone else, just talking about him – is that he's at the top of the tree when it comes to intelligence and being so well read.

'I'll give you an idea. Every football magazine that was around when we were kids, we'd grab it. *Shoot!*, *Match*, whatever he could get his hands on, he would read it cover to cover every week.

'There was one book shop in the city called Melbourne Sports Books. There was a guy who ran it who got to know us pretty well, because we would get the tram into the city as our day out – and we would purchase and devour any football biographies. Our growing up, and him specifically, was all about learning as much as he could.

'I saw the reaction when he got over there [Scotland], the questions about his background. People don't understand that this is a lifetime of him investing everything in football – because he's so interested in it and has such a love for the game. He knows everything about football, things you wouldn't imagine about European football, even though he grew up on the other side of the world. And that's in part down to his intelligence.'

If you wander from South Yarra down to neighbouring Prahran today, you'll find an area of Melbourne full of contrasts. Take one road and you'll find hipster barbers, chic boutiques (is there any other kind?), artisan bakeries and cuisine from all over the Pacific. Take another turning and you're just as likely to pass by down-and-outs hollering across the street at each other. As the great Bill Bryson once said of 1970s Glasgow, it gives the place a certain tang.

There's more than a hint of the old Greek influence about the place, though. The street food available at Prahran Market might be some of the best on the planet, even if you don't go for the 'moussaka just like your grandmother made it', to quote directly from one of the blackboards. Authenticity still has a value in the old neighbourhood.

How authentic, then, is Postecoglou? What is he? A visionary, a prophet, a far-sighted tactician destined to be at the leading edge of innovation? He's surely much more than just a journeyman grafter who, but for superhuman persistence, might still have been coaching the under-11s at Nunawading City FC and picking up punditry shifts on Fox Sports Australia. He might just be that rarest of things in a sport where dumb luck and stupid circumstance play such cruel and crucial roles – a coach whose time has come. At long, long last.

Deligiannis told me a story about being at a business luncheon where he was sitting next to veteran Aussie political journalist Barrie Cassidy, host of a long-running weekend TV show that covers sport as well as current affairs. As talk turned to guests and Ange's name popped up, Cassidy apparently began raving about the quality of his contributions.

Deligiannis, eager to press the 'Renaissance Man' qualities of his friend, said: 'He told me Ange was the kind of guy he loves having on, because he's obviously going to be great on football and has a wide range of knowledge about all sport. But he also said: "I love that he can comment about other stuff, because he's well informed on current affairs, knows what's going on. He's so well read and I love throwing to him, because I know he'll have a comment – even on a subject that most people in sport wouldn't have a clue about." That gives you an indication of what he's like. He's not just a football obsessive.'

That shouldn't come as an enormous surprise, at least not to anyone who has spent time studying the lives of sport's great leaders. Yes, they all devote a truly ridiculous amount of time and effort to mastering their craft; one of the reasons veteran rugby coach Eddie Jones has such a tight bond with Postecoglou is because they're both likely to be found immersing themselves in the latest problem. But you'll often find that the very best have diversions – history, films, music, politics – that keep them sane. In the case of Postecoglou, being aware of major social issues is as natural as breathing. Another thing we can trace back to his family.

It's important, when telling this story, to understand just what life was like for Greek immigrants to Melbourne in the 1970s. What we'd now identify as racism and xenophobia would just be accepted as facts of life back then, Ange writing in his autobiography: 'Folk like us landed laid bare, exposed to the elements. You made do . . . You have to be in such a situation, with no language and no access to the community, to really understand how debilitating it is, how dehumanising it is.'

His dad and his uncle had already worked abroad in construction, venturing to Libya – not the most stable of places, even then – and sending back money to Greece, before deciding that the whole family should up sticks and seek to make a new life for themselves. Once that decision was made, they then had one more choice: Australia or apartheid-era South Africa. Sponsored by a family they didn't even know, and with no grasp of the English language, the Postecoglous took a leap into the unknown. Even if Melbourne was already well on its way to becoming home to the largest Greek diaspora outside of Cyprus, a young Ange always felt like his dad was biding his time in Australia, trying to make enough to return in triumph to the land of his birth.

The struggles of the family would have been familiar to many who made the same transition at a difficult time. In his autobiography, Ange tells a story about his dad and uncle going to collect a mattress someone was giving away, then being unable to find their way home in a city where they couldn't even read the street signs. Think about that for a minute. Stumbling around a foreign land carrying a second-hand mattress. Unable to even ask for directions. It's hard to imagine feeling more lost. And that single incident, on top of all the other struggles, might have been enough to make some give up.

Among those who contributed their personal insight on the Postecoglou family to this book, however, the recurring theme is of Jim's enduring – almost unyielding – toughness, typified by a determination to do whatever it took to make a better life for his family. Young Ange never had to ask just why his dad always seemed exhausted. If there were hours to be worked, Jim took them. So, when he talks about the lack of safety net available to his parents making that gigantic leap of faith from Greece to Australia, it certainly puts into perspective his brave/bold/foolhardy agreement to take the Celtic gig without being allowed to bring in a close pal to act as his assistant. He wasn't raised to shirk from a challenge just because it might cause a bit of discomfort.

Football was always a release for both father and son from the very outset, with Ange saying going to Hellas games meant 'it was like we could breathe'. Even if you go to South Melbourne games now, in 2023, you'll hear Greek being spoken in the clubhouse and find a pretty good lamb souvlaki – fatty in all the right places, with just the perfect amount of tzatziki – at the top of the takeaway menu. Back in the seventies, when every football team in Australia was based on an ethnic immigrant group, it must have been like walking into a bar in Piraeus.

Nicholas Maikousis, the current South Melbourne president, is a contemporary of Postecoglou who was on the board when Ange transitioned from captain to assistant and then head coach. As his name suggests, he shares a Greek heritage with many of the leading figures at a club stubbornly resistant to all official attempts to erase their Hellenic history.

'What would it have been like when Ange first came along with his dad?' asked Maikousis. 'A cauldron. A cauldron of Greeks. But Ange I think was a late migrant here; the majority started to come over here in the 1950s and his parents were a bit later than that. He was born virtually the same time I was. And, when he landed here, this was the home of the Greek community. It really was. They'd get off at Port Melbourne, at Station Pier there and, one way or another, they'd all make their way to Middle Park. There's some footage that we came across probably a month or so ago now of a game at Olympic Park. And there's probably, I'm just guessing, 20–25,000 people. Football was built by migrants here. And there was a place for kids to play. So Ange went all the way through the junior ranks.'

Postecoglou's love for the environment didn't end after the final whistle, either. While the other kids were outside playing at whichever family home the regulars had decanted to for Sunday evening reflections and heated debate, he would sit at a table with his dad and the other old-timers, listening to them dissect the tactics that had contributed to the latest win/loss/draw by the team they loved. It was educational. And, if Jim occasionally told his boy to bugger off outside and play with the other lads, there was always a suspicion that he was pleased when Ange refused to go.

'My desire for my father's attention and company was the precursor to my own love for the game,' is how Postecoglou explains this complex relationship, adding: 'I can't remember a discussion with my father about anything other than football.' The result of this bonding by proxy between father and son? A deeper understanding of the game, born of hours spent listening to the old greybeards explain exactly where Hellas were going wrong. And learning to appreciate just what an important outlet football was for a community of new citizens who, for a very long time, must have felt like they were barely clinging on to the bottom rung of the ladder.

Speaking at a fundraising event back home in 2017, about a year before his father's passing, Postecoglou explained a little more about his understanding of what had taken the family to Australia. It certainly wasn't in pursuit of some freewheeling ride to a mythical promised land.

'The traditional way of talking about it is that people came here for a better life – but my father, I'm convinced he hasn't had a better life,' he was quoted as saying by the Greek-Australian bi-weekly newspaper *Neos Kosmos*. 'He would have had a better life if he stayed at home surrounded by family and friends because whatever hardships he would have gone through, that support would have got him through. I think he came here to give myself and my sister a better life and an opportunity for a better life.'

Explaining a little more about the role played by football, Postecoglou talked movingly about being woken in the middle of the night to watch games being beamed into the family home from some far-flung corner of Europe. As the two men of the house sat in the darkened front room, young Ange liked to pretend that everyone else in the world was asleep. And it's certainly a lovely image, this scene of an over-burdened father passing on his love of the game to a son only too eager to grab at something – anything – capable of lifting the old man out of his seemingly permanent state of stress and exhaustion. In an era when men most certainly did not talk about their feelings, a mutual interest in the game acted as a vehicle for expressing deeper emotions. Nothing says 'I love you' quite as much as giving up precious hours of already limited sleep just to enjoy a shared experience.

Deligiannis, who witnessed all of this at close range, says simply: 'His dad was a huge factor. He says it so many times but it's true – and I saw it unfolding. His dad loved the game and loved to see it played in a certain way. He also, as Ange has said often enough, was someone who was hard to please. No matter how well Ange was doing, and he was doing really well, his dad would always say: "You can do better." So Ange has always had this thing about pleasing his dad. Earning his respect. And doing it in a way he would have appreciated. Jim was a massive influence on Ange, a huge influence on Ange.'

There's more than a hint, in conversations with different people, that Jim was more demanding than even the average immigrant dad working under severe pressure. Rather famously, according to Ange himself, his father's first words to him after the Asian Cup win with Australia were something along the lines of: 'Yeah, but if you'd made a better substitution, you wouldn't have needed extra time . . .' It's a recurring thing, among high achievers, this withholding of parental praise.

There are probably a good few hundred footballers, guys who have worked and toiled under Ange Postecoglou, who could testify to the lasting influence of that approach. As a captain and then a gaffer, he has never been one to go overboard with compliments. Even now, his former Celtic players admit that the man they called gaffer was sparing, in the extreme, with words of praise. Which, of course, makes every plaudit all the more precious to those on the receiving end.

Maikousis, who can still be seen chatting with some of the old Greek-speaking characters on match day at Lakeside Stadium, said: 'You see Ange talk a lot about his father and the fact that outside of football, they probably didn't even communicate. Certainly, he'd be working in the factories, going home in the evenings. The only thing that they really bonded together with was football and South Melbourne.

'Even though that generation were hardened and not too open, when it came to football, it was a little bit different. You probably saw, and I certainly did with my own family, a very different side to our parents and grandparents. There's no question his father was very, very proud of what Ange was achieving.'

When Jim passed away, Maikousis arranged tributes from the club, including – at Ange's request – getting a Hellas scarf draped across the coffin. It's a scene that could be played out in any corner of Planet Football, with devotion to a club recognised as an integral part of many a life well lived. Never let anyone tell you that this is just a game. It's so much more than that.

That's the environment and the community that made Ange the man he is today, then. Noisy, devoted, passionate, committed to the point of fanaticism, joyous and tempestuous according to the bounce of a ball or waving of a linesman's flag. His roots are in Prahran and his heart will always feel the tug of that ex-pat Greek community where his family found a lasting home. Everything he does now remains influenced by those formative years. And one man, in particular.

'I still pretend my father is in the grandstand,' he admitted, to an online gathering of coaches and analysts, talking about the gruff figure who would constantly steer him towards watching the Leeds of Eddie Gray and Peter Lorimer, or the legendary Dutch team who changed the game forever at the 1974 World Cup. 'Would he be enjoying watching this team? That's always been the root of everything I've done. Where it all started from is more powerful than any criticism I'll get. My ideas are so deep-rooted it'll never change.'

Invited to pass on advice to coaches trying to find their own path, their own game model, their own belief system that might help them endure difficult times, awkward bosses or a horrendous run of results, Postecoglou said simply: 'Your philosophy has to come from something within you, reflect who you are as a person. You're not going to shift Diego Simeone, Jürgen Klopp or Pep Guardiola on what they believe. And their beliefs aren't just from something they've seen, but something within them. It starts with understanding who you are as a person, the kind of coach you want to be. You'll find the philosophy and system that suits you.

'The one thing you know is, when you go into a dressing room full of people that potentially you've never met before, people are pretty good at seeing someone who is genuine – and someone who is just doing something because they're mimicking somebody else. They'll test your beliefs, test who you are. If what you're saying isn't coming from deep inside you, you'll second-guess yourself. It's not about copying anyone else.

'If you say you want your team to play like Pep Guardiola but your inner soul is Diego Simeone, you're passionate and you want your team to fight, want your teams to battle, at some point there is going to be a disconnect. When you are under pressure, you will fall back on who you are. And players will say: "Hold on a minute, you wanted us to play possession football, now you want us to do something entirely different."

'I was lucky. My philosophy came when I was five years old, holding my dad's hand, walking into the football and looking up at the most powerful person in my life.'

As true as that may be, no one goes through life without evolving. Conversations with people who were actually on the scene for major turning points in Postecoglou's life – from pitting his wits against Sir Alex Ferguson's Manchester United at the FIFA World Club Championship to leaving his youth job with Soccer Australia in pretty dismal circumstances – give the impression of someone who learned to adapt to different situations. He's rolled with a few heavy blows and, when he's been knocked down, found a way to get back on his feet. Through it all, he's kept faith with a philosophy in the proudest traditions of the beautiful game. Stayed true to his father's principles. And become very much his own man.

Key Game

AUSTRALIA 2 NETHERLANDS 3

World Cup Group B
18 June 2014

MADE it. Top of the world? Not quite. But this felt like the culmination of a long, long journey for a coach who set himself the ambition, at a very young age, of managing at the biggest tournament on earth. And facing the Dutch? Well, that carried extra resonance, given the role played by their wonderful World Cup squad of 1974 in his own development as a football fan. Rinus Michels' team – Cruyff, Neeskens, the Van de Kerkhof brothers et al. – were considered almost demi-gods by Jim Postecoglou; it was only natural that they'd become his son's reference point on matters of faith in Total Football.

The fact that Australia lost all three group games in Brazil, a 3–1 defeat by Chile and a 3–0 scudding by defending champions Spain falling either side of the Dutch match, came as no shock to anyone. The Socceroos were not expected to achieve anything at the tournament; it's one of the things Postecoglou wanted to change, in the long term, about Australia's approach.

Naturally, he would have preferred to have won a game. Squirrelled away a point or two. Shown the world that the Aussies weren't just along for the party.

When he thinks back on the experience, though, Postecoglou's mind is inevitably drawn to something that happened before the tournament even kicked off. The day of the draw, to be precise. And a text message from then teenage son, James. Admitting that he fully expected to see something rude/cheeky/insulting, Ange opened up his phone to find that the kid had simply said: 'Here's your chance to become a legend.' Fathers, sons and football, eh? A potent mix down the generations.

Chapter 2

O CAPTAIN, MY CAPTAIN

UNITED by a common language and a love of go-forward football intended to run ragged any opposition fool enough to expect even half a heartbeat of respite, the Galloping Major and the overlapping/underlapping/always attacking young full back were certainly kindred spirits. The legendary Ferenc Puskás, who led South Melbourne to four major trophies during his three years as manager, never found club captain Ange Postecoglou – his unofficial chauffeur, translator and apprentice – anything less than eager to lap up any advice, experience or wisdom he felt like passing on. It's hardly surprising that many a friend and former teammate detects a hint of the Puskás philosophy in much of what Postecoglou has achieved as a manager.

It's important to note, however, that influences are just that. Vectors likely to affect the trajectory of a career, a path, a life. Some carry more weight than others; a few are large enough to generate their own gravitational field. But success in football isn't guaranteed for anyone falling into the orbit of a super-massive intellect. Nobody makes it in this game simply by wholesale adoption of another gaffer's game model.

To get an idea of the forces that shaped Postecoglou as a coach, then, you have to look at the entirety of his playing career. The transition from promising newcomer to undisputed leader on the pitch. The pressures that inevitably followed his ascension to the captaincy – at just 22 years old – of an institution held in almost religious regard by Melbourne's devoted Greek community. The relentless push to improve conditions and raise expectations of everyone at 'his' club. And, crucially for anyone trying to develop the emotional intelligence needed to lead any group, learning to tailor his message to suit the audience, acting as a conduit between dressing room and boardroom.

Any visitor to South Melbourne's Lakeside ground, a pleasant enough community stadium – despite the athletics track – that is also home to 'Combat Australia's National Performance Centre', quickly learns just how enormous a figure Postecoglou is in the story of a club stubbornly clinging on to its position of historical influence, despite the best corporate efforts to rid Aussie football of its ethnic backstory. He's front and centre of the painting commissioned to mark the club's Team of the Century, where he fills the left back berth. Current club president Nicholas Maikousis is only half joking when he tells Ange – frequently – that he was probably lucky to make the starting line-up. Although he does qualify this by insisting that Postecoglou should have pipped Manny Poulakakis in the poll for head coach of this fantasy team.

Look down the honours board at Lakeside and you'll see that, standing apart from a healthy collection of cup wins and regional competition victories, they boast four National Soccer League titles. Postecoglou was captain for two of those, in 1984 and 1991. And manager for the back-to-back triumphs in 1998 and 1999. Few have made a greater contribution. Starting with his first-team breakthrough as a 17-year-old.

Old team-mates recall a player who used to bomb forward from the left back position. A guy who bristled against the need to work in a bank to supplement his meagre part-time pay at South. An Aussie bloke proud of his Greek heritage and capable of conversing with the old-time supporters – and directors – in their native tongue. A character who took to the captaincy naturally enough, whether that be raising important issues with the board or arranging end-of-season jolly boys' outings to some truly glamorous locations. And, of course, a footballing anorak with an inexhaustible appetite for information on the game he loved.

To paint a picture of just how big South Melbourne were when Ange was coming through the ranks, just take a look at some of the names recruited as manager over the years. A few years before Postecoglou broke through as a player, the great Tommy Docherty – a former Manchester United and Scotland boss who also happened to be one of the game's great raconteurs – was lured Down Under to take charge for a season. This was a club who always seemed to find big money, relatively speaking, to attract celebrity coaching talent from abroad or hoover up the best gaffers on the Australian scene. Postecoglou was promoted into the first-team squad by the late Len McKendry, mastermind of that 1984 title and regarded as one of the finest coaches in the history of the Australian game, then served under club legend John Margaritis, before taking instruction from

Puskás – the magical Magyar whose expansive attacking game delivered Grand Final glory in 1991 – and finally Frank Arok, who made the skipper his assistant when injury brought the defender's playing career to a premature end.

In terms of glamour and gravitas, of course, none of the managers who came and went during Postecoglou's playing days could hold a candle to Puskás, whose arrival in 1989 represented a truly remarkable piece of recruitment by the South Melbourne board. Universally regarded as one of the greatest footballers ever to lace up boots, his exploits with Real Madrid and Hungary inspiring a rare degree of global fame in a game on the cusp of a new era, the great man's name still adorns the FIFA award for the year's most beautiful goal in world football. Never quite the same force as a manager, he was hardly some no-hoper cashing in on his playing reputation when he took the Melbourne offer. After all, under his management, Panathinaikos had reached the European Cup Final at Wembley in 1971, the all-Greek squad losing to a legendary Ajax team – Cruyff, Neeskens et al. – completing the first leg of their hat-trick in football's most prestigious club competition. Think of landing Puskás, then, as the equivalent to the current South board persuading Zinedine Zidane to take charge for their crack at life in the National Second Tier.

That was certainly the case in terms of attention generated. Postecoglou has spoken about how this period in his playing career gave him a first glimpse of what genuine sporting celebrity looked like; the sight of parents thrusting babies into the arms of the smiling old gent, before reaching for their cameras, underlined the euphoria capable of being generated by this silly little kids' game. Growing up, he'd already fallen under the spell of the odd superstar himself, idolising former Arsenal forward Charlie George and Newcastle United legend Malcolm 'Supermac' Macdonald during their brief stints in the old National Soccer League. But, with Puskás, there was a realisation that such devotion wasn't inspired merely by his medal count, impressive though it may have been. It was the swagger of the man. The fact that he had always been synonymous with flair and adventure, in a game always caught on the horns of a struggle between pragmatism and purist pursuit of excitement.

Postecoglou, who had been a ball boy at Middle Park and a leader all the way through the youth ranks, was arguably the perfect captain for any new manager to inherit. Someone who innately understood both the ambitions and limitations of the club. That fact that Puskás could fall back on the Greek he learned at Panathinaikos whenever his limited grasp of English failed him, knowing that the skipper would step in to translate, was an added bonus. For both.

'Ange used to pick Puskás up and drive him to training,' said former South stalwart Steve Blair, already established at centre half when this Postecoglou kid joined the first-team group. 'Of course, Ange would pick his brains. He'd be talking about this and that. Puskás didn't really care for people like me, a centre half, a defender, don't worry about them. He was just all attack, attack, attack! But Ange was a sponge for any information he could gather. You have to look at all these influences on Ange. If you understand from here, how he's got to where he is now, playing the system that he is playing, it's no secret. Because he's been indoctrinated with this from the greatest.'

For his part, Postecoglou puts Puskás second only to his own father in the degree of influence he had on his career. He speaks with a mix of affection and wonder about how he used to ferry the living legend around in 'my crappy old car'. Not that Puskás ever complained about getting lifts to training in a banger that had seen better days; everyone who was at Melbourne during that era stresses the humility of a man who had every right to make big-time demands and act the diva.

In terms of the football played under Puskás, well, even the uber-adventurous Ange used to get a little bit frustrated about the manager's insistence that both wingers should stay high and wide, leaving the full backs open to being overrun. Though he did enjoy being encouraged to join the attack himself. Something his old team-mates can laugh about now.

Former Socceroos captain Paul Wade let out a guffaw as he recalled: 'As a team-mate, it's interesting, because Ange played as a full back. And he loved getting forward. But wasn't so interested in getting back to defend. How times have changed, eh? All right, Ange, we'll get back for you, ya miserable bastard . . . but he was such a good captain. There were times when you wouldn't know he was on the park.'

That doesn't sound, it is suggested, like an ideal quality for someone wearing the armband. Even the least imposing of captains have a way of making their presence known, surely? Wade, who skippered the Socceroos on 66 occasions in an international career that saw him make 113 appearances in the green and gold, is quick to clarify.

'Let me explain,' he said. 'Ange didn't go around shouting and screaming. In the dressing room, some captains feel they have to shout and scream to motivate people. Most of us in that era were very quiet – and he never made himself any louder. When he said something, though, we didn't bow to him . . . but we generally thought: "Yeah, good point. We'll take that on board. We'll go with that." He had a lot of respect from all of his team-mates. He was a man of very few words but the impact he had was real. And it was relatable. I've had captains where you're sitting there thinking: "Oh, shut the f . . ." But with Ange you never did. And the way he interacted with not only the board but someone like Ferenc Puskás was remarkable. He could talk to Puskás like they'd been besties for years and years.'

Like many of his former team-mates, Wade speaks with genuine warmth about Postecoglou's conscientious dedication to the duties that went with captaincy of an old and established club like South Melbourne, whether that be making representations to the board about facilities, bonuses or training arrangements – or taking on the really important stuff, like the annual end-of-season trip. Everyone who was on the famous boys' holiday to Hawaii talks about it in almost mythical terms. Postecoglou always had that ability to straddle two worlds – to smarten himself up for discussions with directors, while not merely appearing to be one of the lads, but genuinely keeping their best interests at heart.

Wade, laughing again at the memory of Ange relentlessly digging him up about his less-than-prolific record in front of goal, explained: 'He could talk to the board but be one of the players, be a yobbo! Not many people can have respect on so many fronts. There are a lot of people who say they need respect on and off the park. Well, he knew when to pull on the reins and say: "No, enough's enough. We need to knuckle down and get to work." And, when it was appropriate, he would say: "Right, boys, let's have some fun." It was, as I say, a beautiful balancing act.

'He used to call me Rushy, after Ian Rush, because I couldn't score in a brothel, never mind a football pitch. He used to take the piss and ask: "Hey, Rushy. Have you given up scoring for Lent?" That's a bit harsh! But even that banter said: "I know how to deal with people. I have emotional intelligence." He was first class at handling people. That's why everyone jumps on his bandwagon, because they all want to be part of it.

'In terms of the actual football, his attitude, as captain, was that the opposition might score eight, but we'll score nine. He always had that attitude. No matter what the score was, we were going to score one more than the opposition. Now, he wasn't satisfied if we conceded seven . . . but he'd hope we'd score eight. And he'd certainly give us enough licence, enough encouragement and enough freedom to go and bang in eight goals at the other end. It was an absolute joy to be part of Puskás and Ange's team for the first few years.'

Joy. That's the overriding theme of any conversation with those who played under the Puskás-Postecoglou leadership team at South, with Blair saying: 'Totally an amazing experience, working with Puskás. Somebody of his quality, I don't know what he must've thought when he came in and trained us. I remember once we had a really early start and we had shooting practice. We had to knock the ball into him, he'd knock it back to us, and we'd shoot. They were going everywhere – over the bar, left and right side, hitting the corner flags – and then he showed us, he stopped us all. He couldn't run as he was quite heavy at the time, but his left peg, you know what I mean? We laid the ball off to him and bang! Top corner. More than that, his humility. He was a really down-to-earth person.

'And his football? It was all attacking, all goals. His knowledge was very high, but his communication wasn't the best. That's why Ange helped as well; Ange could speak to him in Greek. Tactically, Ange was gone as a full back. Just give him the ball and he'd attack, he'd just go. And we'd be left. He'd just go, and go, and go, and go. We were one of the better teams, so more predominantly we would always score and have a lot more attacking play. And Puskás was always into us about shooting and scoring: "If they score two, we'll score four. If we get a chance, just shoot!" All these things have been influences on him.

'Of course, we all wanted to sit next to Puskás when we would fly for interstate games, because that meant he couldn't get away from us. He would have to talk to you! I would always ask him about Celtic and he would always mention Jimmy Johnstone. In broken English, but he would say, "champion", "what a player", and all that. In those times you would be in his ear. Everyone would ask him about winning the European Cup but he was never boastful about it. He'd just seen it all, done it all.

'If you look at the year we won the championship with Puskás, there was a crowd of about 18,000 – which is big for us – and the whole stadium and the players are going nuts, but he's just sitting there as cool as a cucumber. As if: "This is nothing. I don't know what you're all getting excited about." When you think about it, the pitches he's played on, the games he's played in, the importance of the things he's done, to do this in Australia, it's nothing.'

If Puskás could be blasé about even a Grand Final victory, there was nothing equivocal about the support South Melbourne – even without the Hellas tag – enjoyed in a Greek community who cherished their club. There was a very southern European fervour surrounding the organisation, with the ex-pat community clinging to this little piece of home during good times and bad. That generated enormous support, of course. And high expectations.

The landscape of Australian football at the time was all about the 'ethnic' teams. Croatians and Italians, Macedonians and Poles, they all brought their love of the game with them when they landed in the new world. Yet, among those supporter bases, there was also a deep affection and respect for the English game. Part of that was down to exposure, with live matches from the old First Division more likely to be on TV than anything from the Greek top flight. But punters of all backgrounds and origins also fell for the raw excitement that surrounded clubs like Liverpool, Manchester United and – for a spell, anyway – Leeds, all of whom can boast supporters' club branches in Australia to this day.

That indoctrination in the British game meant a steady stream of Home Nations players – either those who had moved out to Australia with their families as kids, or genuine imports leaping at the chance of a different life experience – could be found filling key positions at all clubs. The history of the game in Australia is shot through, for instance, with Scots. Some of whom went on to represent their adopted country.

For those who grew up in the communities where the clubs were founded, of course, being part of 'their' team definitely carried more prestige. And greater pressure. Postecoglou was always going to be a fans' favourite? Sure. If he delivered.

Long-time friend Blair, a man with proud Scottish roots and Celtic in his blood, pointed out: 'He talks about the connection football gave him with his dad. Aye, that's fine. But he could've played and been shite! If he hadn't made the team, maybe nothing would've happened. He came into the team as a young Greek boy but the team was predominantly of British heritage. In fact, he used to be the ball boy when I was playing. Crazy, isn't it? Absolutely crazy. He came in and he was a good player. Young, enthusiastic, skilful, attacking, you know what I mean? Not so much defending! But he did well. And it was a source of immense pride for him. Because it's not like me – Scottish heritage – playing for a Greek club with a Greek badge on it. I was loyal and was there a long time because they were good to me. But, for a Greek boy playing for a Greek club, his dad would've been bursting with pride, which he was. It was a matter of pride for the Greek community.

'That helped him when he got the captaincy. A Greek boy playing for a Greek club and now you're captain of the club? It's a lot of prestige but also a lot of responsibility because there's a lot of pressure on him to do things. He was often caught in between things with players. Ange was always in the middle between the committee, who were all Greek, and the players. He could see it from both sides. And he was always willing to listen.'

If there is no established instruction manual on how to do the captain's role, with every leader having to incorporate their own qualities, quirks and foibles to other people's expectations of how a skipper *should* act, it's equally true that no one has ever written a definitive guide on how to deal with the inevitable and inescapable enemy stalking every athlete: retirement. Cruciate ligament injuries, the root cause of many a career being cut short, eventually did for Ange. Even if it took him a while to realise that he was done. In his own autobiography, he calls his playing career 'a frustration' because of all the things he didn't get a chance to achieve. And he expresses genuine dismay that, as he limped around Middle Park for the South Under-20s on a Sunday morning, an over-age player vainly attempting to regain a mobility lost forever to the scar tissue in and around his knee, nobody had the balls just to tell him that he was finished.

Watching all of this unfold was a young Tim Schleiger, effectively signed as a replacement for the left back who had lost so many of the tools needed to compete in first-team football. Schleiger, who now runs his own physiotherapy and sports science business, remembers a generous, experienced professional who did his best to help the new kid settle in. Even if it meant watching him steal 'his' place in the team.

'He was finishing up and I was coming into his position,' said Schleiger, whose own playing career was also cut short by injury, ironically enough, inspiring him to take up a new profession. Choosing some typically sharp dressing-room language as he explained some of the obstacles faced by any aspiring pro trying to make the grade, he added: 'I talk a lot about football – and football's the same because I'm still involved in football around the world – and how, when you're a young boy coming in, you've got people in the squad who are complete bastards, which is to harden you up. Then you've got one or two genuinely great guys like Steve Blair, for instance. Blairy was the older fellow; he and I just got along like a house on fire. He kept an eye on me and, sort of, kept my football super simple. "So listen, big man, all you've got to do is this and this," is all I'd ever get from him. Or I'd get: "Easy, tiger . . . easy!"

'With Ange, well, as soon as you did your ACL, it was a bit of a life sentence back then, not like today, because you would miss 12 months just doing rehab. And for Ange, he lost four yards of pace. With my physio and conditioning knowledge now, I look back and just go: "Yeah, he recovered but he's stiff. Never got his range back. Never got his speed back." And so, pretty much, that was him done. But he was great with me, and I remember him giving me a lot of advice along the way. I always said that this bloke was going to be a way better coach than he was a player.

'Now, there's a story that he got made Frank Arok's assistant because the team were doing a running trial, a doggies thing, and basically Frank told him that if he came last, he'd have to become his assistant. Ange was the best guy, one of the best players, but he couldn't run by this stage, the poor bastard. He came last by a country mile, so that was the joke that, because he came last in this race, he ended up having to be assistant coach to Frank – which is about the best thing that could've happened to him.'

It's probably best to take that story with a pinch or two of salt. Plenty of people will tell you that Ange was set on coaching from the moment he realised the legs wouldn't do what the brain demanded any more. Even during his playing days, he'd been more influential than your average captain. There was always a feeling, among team-mates, that he wasn't just passing on instructions from the boss. He understood the thinking behind every tactic. Knew when a little bit of extra explanation might help, too.

'What made him special was his insight,' said Schleiger. 'He could spend two minutes with you, but you'd feel like he'd spent half an hour with you. He hit the nail on the head around, you know, six or seven insightful points in two minutes. Football is full of stories of coaches not getting the message through. I've played for a gaffer and never really had a conversation with him for the entire season, just did my job and only really heard from him in team talks. That's what we did. Whereas Ange could spend three or four minutes with you, even just two minutes, and you'd realise you've gone away with three or four things you can use to really improve yourself as a player and a person. I could recognise that as a 17-year-old, that this guy had something special about him.'

Those skills honed as captain would be useful when Arok invited the broken-down left back to join his coaching set-up, the former Socceroos boss recognising the value of retaining someone who had served his apprenticeship under some really interesting gaffers. Including one of the greatest names in the history of the game. Arok might also have felt it was useful to add a proper South Melbourne man to his team. Someone who understood the culture of the organisation. And who could be relied upon to do the right thing for 'his' club, whenever duty called.

Chapter 3

INSPIRED BY HURT – ANGE'S GOLDEN RULES

WHEN you're in a hurry to make a mark, only absolute commitment to a course of action will do. Caution and pragmatism rarely feature, after all, in tales of heroic derring-do. When the leading man just happens to be closer to 60 than 50 and has devoted his entire adult life to reaching the foothills of his own personal Everest, enduring shattering setbacks and devastating disasters along the way, hesitation so close to the summit would represent a betrayal of all that effort. Even shifting into a lower gear isn't an option for Ange Postecoglou, a man who genuinely wondered if the biggest opportunities had forever passed him by.

How to explain this onwards, ever onwards philosophy? Start by understanding that, according to long-time assistant and confidant Peter Cklamovski, his old gaffer genuinely believes he can be 'one of the best managers in the world'. A long list of players who had their careers transformed, revitalised or resuscitated by Postecoglou will gladly line up to testify on his behalf, with many citing his courage in implementing revolutionary (for the time and place, certainly) tactics and ideas, certain that it would yield rewards. Among those who know him best, everything he's achieved in recent years feels like vindication of that belief. And long overdue payback for some heavy falls taken on the way up.

So, yes, Postecoglou's approach to football, tactics and the absolute truths of management represents the very antithesis of that old Groucho Marx quote: 'These are my principles. And, if you don't like them, well, I have others . . .' He is unyielding in what he does, sticking to the master plan when everyone around him, from the cheap seats to the directors' box, is urging the sort of compromise that might, just might, nick you a result in a game against superior opposition. Part of his constancy is rooted in a deeply held belief that improvement is only possible if players continue to express themselves in an open and expansive manner. Even if it means taking the odd shellacking along the way. But there's much more to this thrawn streak that keeps Ange faithful to the golden rules of attacking, quick, explosive football designed to cause problems for the opponent.

Some of the motivation can be traced back to childhood and a simple desire to play in a style guaranteed to gladden the heart of his own father. Never underestimate the craving for parental approval as a motivating factor in life; history is littered with examples of men – and it is mostly men – moving mountains in the hope of provoking a smile from some stern authoritarian figure from their early life. As many of his friends readily testify, in this case, that sort of obligation doesn't go away simply because said figure is no longer around to bestow their blessing in person.

Yet there's another, equally powerful force propelling Postecoglou along this path, too. Call it a pent-up sense of frustration at being made to wait until recently, well into his sixth decade on earth, to land a job truly commensurate with his ability. He waited forever to reach the Champions League. When he got there, well, Ange was simply channelling his inner Jerry Lee Lewis. If you've seen the highly enjoyable *Great Balls of Fire* biopic of the strong-willed American rock 'n' roll pioneer, you'll remember the scene where he tells his pious, God-fearing, evangelical, forever sermonising cousin: 'If I'm going to hell, I'm going there playing the piano.' In Ange's case, he was never going to waste time by rolling back on ideals, striking some ugly deal with the devil in exchange for a hard-fought nil-nil away to Real Madrid. If he's going to suffer a defeat, he'll do it his way.

Cklamovski, who spent the best part of a decade and a half learning that there was no point in arguing with Ange, is clear on exactly why his old boss has refused to waver, regardless of circumstance, the boss of Japanese club FC Tokyo explaining: 'There was a long time where he probably thought, deep down, that he'd missed the boat. And I think he said it publicly, that this was a chance he might have missed out on.

'And all of this, this is hurt. This is pain. Because he truly believes in himself that he is one of the best managers in the world – or can be one of the best managers in the world. And all this heartache tests belief, tests character. You can see the manager he is now – that doesn't happen just with one straight line, obviously. He's been through a lot. Thirty years of his coaching career has got him to this point.

'His football has always been a certain way; the intent and belief has always been a certain way. His staff and his coaches get refined along with the evolution of it and that will never stop.

'It's not just the way it looks. When I say that, I believe this too, he loves watching it, he loves watching his team play. That's everything for him. But it's successful. Get the football right and success can follow.

'It's well documented why that's important to him and that goes deeper. To his father. Building teams that his father would like to play in, and respect to his father for that. Ange being the great man he is, everything [is] for his father, right? But, beyond that, it is the football that he loves and the football he believes in. If you get it right, and when you get it right, he knows how to build it to get success.'

Different formations have come and gone during the three decades since Postecoglou first took up a coaching gig at South Melbourne. All sorts of tactics have fallen in and out of fashion, as football transitioned through trends and innovations, regressions and revelations. Back threes, flat fours, midfield sitters, double pivots, pressing as a quasi-religious way of life, strict positional play versus fluid rotations intended to make opponents dizzy . . . all successful coaches take elements of the latest fad that work for them. The key is knowing what to select. And what to discard.

But what we saw at Celtic was the culmination of a lifetime love affair with a specific sort of soccer. The fascination with seeing the game played in a certain way means he has embraced – or even pioneered – ideas like pushing his full backs into midfield and freeing his attacking midfielders to run the channels in a full five-lane attack. Get the timing spot-on and it's guaranteed to stretch any defence to break-ing point. You can trace this evolution all the way back to the beginning of his coaching career. Earlier than that, even, to his time as a South Melbourne player under the legendary Ferenc Puskás. Drop in on almost any point along the way of his timeline and you'll find evidence of 'Ange-ball' DNA somewhere in every team, every season, every player recruited, discarded, transformed or inspired to embrace a new and bold approach to this game of fine margins and fighting for every yard.

To pigeonhole Postecoglou as merely a possession junkie, one of those coaches who can only see the game through one specific statistic, would be to misjudge his approach entirely, with the man himself always wary of simply keep-ing the ball. He talks with disdain about getting into a seemingly comfortable rhythm that fails to threaten the opposition. And he continually stresses the importance of creating overloads in the final third, then striking with the sort of rapidity that would leave a mongoose flat-footed.

In his world, the ball can go forward quickly, certainly. A centre half with good distribution skills will be encouraged, in fact, to find a mobile forward early, if that's what the situation requires. But there's no simply shelling aimless punts into the opposition half in the hope of turning defenders and making them face their own goal. And, when it comes to breaking forward, Postecoglou wants his teams to go all-in, throwing bodies into that magical final third and flooding danger zones with intent. Damn the risks. Focus on those rewards.

Against teams who sit deep in possession – that would be ten out of the other 11 teams in the Scottish Premiership, a fact of footballing life that seems to upset some fans whenever it's mentioned – there was a premium on drawing the back four/five/six out in pursuit of the ball. That area just in front and just behind the final line of defence? That's the golden zone for Ange. The area where his rotations and well-rehearsed phases of play come off. And also the place where his players feel free to try things out. His teams will vary the pace, sure, in a bid to get a better look at the opposition defence. When they decide to hit the accelerator, though, they're tough to contain.

Within that overall game model, there has been a natural evolution and development of ideas. When he guided Australia to the World Cup in 2014, the Socceroos didn't stray too far from a 4-2-3-1 formation that relied on Tim Cahill as a focal point up front, with full backs pushing forward and two holding midfielders providing a solid rest defence to guard against the counter-attack. Yet Postecoglou shifted to a 3-4-2-1 in qualification for the 2018 World Cup in Russia because it got the most out of midfielders like Tom Rogic and Aaron Mooy. He's not bound by dogma.

In the couple of seasons before joining Spurs, he seemed to have settled on an expansive 4-3-3 that is both a throwback to a golden age of Total Football – and an example of where the game has been heading in recent times. Creating width to get gaps in the middle has been a dominant trend in the Champions League and, with the high press gradually giving way to medium or low blocks, Postecoglou's game – honed at Yokohama, who are of course members of the City Football Group – has a cutting-edge look about it. That he wasn't tempted to rein back on his ambitions, even when leading Celtic into the Santiago Bernabéu, is no surprise to those who have seen this particular movie play out in a few different settings now.

Thomas Broich, the former Brisbane Roar star who went on to become a respected tactical expert in his native Germany, most recently in his role as Head of Methodology at Hertha Berlin, remains struck by the style his old boss brought to an A-League still leaning heavily on an outdated British model as the 2010s rolled around. He moved half-way across the world because Postecoglou sold him on his vision, after all. The guy certainly talked a good enough game to get Broich on the plane. What really impressed him, though, was the balls it took for Ange to persist when all around were losing their heads. A trait that continues to this very day.

'To me, the single most important thing that I've come to realise over the years because I talk about it so much, it wasn't about the football side of things, I think it was courage and bravery,' said Broich. 'Yeah, his style of football is great, his tactical knowledge is outstanding, his design of drills is second to none, he ticks all those boxes. To me, the key ingredient always was that he was very uncompromising and very, very brave.

'Imagine you're coaching an Australian football team and they're pretty much used to playing an English-style 4-4-2, playing off second balls and channel balls. And then his approach is: "We're going to play like Barcelona, basically. We'll try just short passes; pass and move, pass and move."

'When you first start with that kind of approach, you're in all sorts of trouble. It's not going to work overnight. To have the capacity to endure all that, to go through that rough patch, to keep believing, to instil that kind of belief; that is an enormous task and, to me, that's probably the key quality.

'A lot of coaches have similar ideas. Ideally, they want to play that brand of football, but they do not have the guts to go through with it. He did that at every club despite early challenges.

'It was the same at Celtic, right? At one point I was worried for him at a distance, because I think they had three losses, one draw and three wins after seven games, I thought they might sack him – you have to be so brave to go through that.'

Recalling how he'd been convinced to leave the Bundesliga for a new life in Australia, specifically the meeting where Postecoglou had persuaded him to sign on for a great adventure, Broich said: 'Yeah, I was playing at Nürnberg at the time, and he was on a scouting trip across Europe. We had a little date and he drove over from Belgium that day, so that would have been a little eight-hour trip – one way, mind you! We had a bit of a sit-down and talked.

'To be honest with you, in the beginning, I liked the guy, I liked his vision of football but, you know, a lot of people can talk the talk in football, so it didn't make much of a difference – like, yeah, this is interesting; I want to leave the club; this is an opportunity for me to play football abroad; to get a chance to fall in love with football again, which was really important for me at that stage; and the picture he was painting of the football he was going to play, it suited me. To be honest with you, I did not give it much thought at the time.'

It's fair to say that the bright lights of Brisbane didn't feature in the daydreams of many European footballers with options to stay closer to home, Broich laughing as he recalled: 'Australia in terms of football was a bit like a Third World country. And it was only when we actually got to work, and I got to experience him on a daily basis, when I realised this guy is *the* big deal.

'To this day, he is, by far, the best coach I've ever had. And I said that from that time on, even ten years ago when nobody was talking about him – even here in Germany, I told them of this guy in Australia, but nobody had heard of him. He's such a master of football; he's a coaching genius.

'It did not start straight away; it took a whole pre-season and a few games to get going. But, with Ange it's always the way you reach that tipping point and I guess once the whole thing really gets going, once you develop momentum, then you realise this could be something special.'

There's a missionary zeal about many of those who have worked with Postecoglou. In researching this book, there has been a recurring theme of true believers, ardent disciples, lining up to explain just why their guy might be one of the most inspirational leaders in sport. He must be doing something right.

The man himself believes that coaching is about more than just winning titles. The prospect of going into a club and changing things for the long term will always prove enticing for someone who, in his own autobiography/manifesto, wrote the sentence: 'I am a coach who enjoys climbing mountains. I am a coach who must climb mountains.'

That's some statement. And it cuts to the heart of why he does what he does. Because he is compelled. It's not a choice. He couldn't just settle into a role and protect what he has. His skin would itch and his eyes water at the very thought. Possibly because he remembers the one period of his life when outside influences forced him on to the back foot. It did not end well.

Postecoglou was sacked as head coach of the Young Socceroos in 2007, after seven years of working and sweating inside Football Australia's youth system, following their failure to qualify for the FIFA Under-20 World Cup. It was a brutal time for him, working against a backdrop of stagnating talent development across the senior game in Australia. His discomfort was laid bare in a famous televised argument with former international-turned-pundit Craig Foster, covered in more detail later in this book.

Looking back on that period a few years later, by which stage he'd re-established himself as Brisbane Roar coach and was again earning praise as one of the most respected leaders in the game, Postecoglou himself admitted: 'Towards the end, it was probably the only time in my life when I thought too much about job preservation. Whether it was to appease certain people or whether it was the pressure, I compromised. The lesson I learnt was that I could never be successful if I compromised my beliefs. When I left, I said to myself: "The next job I get I'll be dogmatic; no one will tell me what to do any more." I know all about the Aussie tall poppy syndrome, but nobody's going to put me in a box. If I want to say something, I'll say it. Basically, I don't give a shit about what people think of me any more.'*

With that one exception, Postecoglou believes he's followed these principles all the way up the ladder, embarking on an adventure, building something unique. And

---

* *Sydney Morning Herald* interview, 3 December 2011

taking players along with him. He's no self-help guru just trying to spew out positive catchphrases. His man management style – distant in the extreme – owes plenty to the old-school approaches of a generation who would deliberately ignore players in order to keep them on edge. Yet he definitely recognises how the game has changed since his own first forays into the first team, as a nervous 17-year-old too frightened to open his mouth.

In practical terms, that means that he explains his thinking. Because he wants converts, not automatons. So, while he'll always prefer to keep explanations simple, and he actively discourages players from getting too familiar with him on a personal level, he conveys a message of being not only in total control of the situation – but genuinely dedicated to helping these footballers achieve greatness.

He knows, incidentally, that shouting from the technical area has limited impact in any game. For him, half-time has always been key. The purest distillation of a manager's job. By his own estimation, once everyone is in the dressing room, he has maybe four minutes to get his message across. At a time when players' heads are spinning, when he himself might be suffering sensory overload as information comes at him from all angles, he has to gauge the psychology of the group and the different emotional state of individuals. All while remembering one golden rule of coaching: Don't fuck this up.

But the half-time pointers, the pre-game reminders, Matchday-1 analysis sessions and the detailed game plans – none of them would work in isolation. To build something as intricate as Postecoglou has, with different teams in wildly different footballing environments, from South Melbourne to Japan's second city just south of Tokyo, from Patras to Glasgow and now, he hopes, London, requires a constant effort. Every. Single. Day. Without a minute being wasted.

Speaking to people from different stages of his career, it quickly becomes clear that there are a couple of ways any player can piss the man off. Top of the list is straying from the game plan. Followed closely by taking too many safe options for fear of making a costly mistake. More than one former player or coach provides anecdotal evidence of Ange going out of his way to protect – and even praise – a defender who has cost his team a goal because he tried to play out from the back, in accordance with instructions. On days when the back four and midfield have struggled with their passing into the opposition red zone, he's flipped the situation around by criticising strikers for not making more intelligent runs to open up space. Standard managerial psychology? Maybe. But it also speaks to his role as a leader. He wants players to understand the bigger picture, to recognise the importance of their role but also to appreciate the difficulties likely to be faced by their team-mates 10, 20 or 50 yards away on the pitch. All of that takes time and effort.

Cklamovski, asked to identify key elements of his old gaffer's game model, says simply: 'I'll answer it with three words that became synonymous with Ange and Celtic's campaign: "We never stop." It's spot on. That's the intent behind it, so yes, it's the football that he loves and believes in. He gets the group galvanised to go in a certain direction with that football from when the first whistle goes until full time and then you recover, and you do it again the next day and the day after that.

'What's important with that, and how that gets built in, is the daily process. The game model is clear: "They want to attack a certain way" or "they want to defend a certain way" – it's all connected. It's a strong football model. Equally important is what gets coached into players daily. And I think that's the weapon, it's mentality. Mentality coming from Ange, his inspiring words and, on a daily basis, it's the high standards coming from everyone around Ange as well – his assistant coaches and every support staff around him. It's a mentality environment. Coaching that mentality into the players on a daily basis – and that's connected to the football they play as well. That's why you see some epic last-minute wins, or late goals, or nil–nils turning into one–nils. Or five-nils because they get that goal, and it never stops because that says everything about the football that gets built on daily – both from a football and mentality perspective.

'It's all based on playing a brand of football that everyone fell in love with at Celtic, obviously. The key mantra for him was to play football that gets everyone excited and gets the fans off their seats. And so, if you want to play like that on the weekend, you've got to train a lot every day. Obviously, I think it's fair to say, the evolution from the starting point to 15 years or so later is a really exciting evolution of a game model that's really clear and distinct. And that gets put into practice and into place every day. Players love it, staff love it, and the fans love it on the weekend.'

Laughing at the very idea that Postecoglou might be tempted to temper his approach against even the very best teams on the planet, Cklamovski points to Champions

League encounters with Real Madrid (eight goals conceded, one scored across two group games that saw Celtic receive plenty of plaudits for daring to take on the reigning La Liga champions) and says: 'The objective is to control and dominate.

'In his career, he started in different ways in terms of formations and the essence of controlling a game. It's all based on being as attacking as possible, scoring as many goals as possible and, genuinely, getting the fans excited to come back next game. That's the essence of it.

'His belief has been tested in the toughest circumstances. I know everyone is talking about – and it's a credit to Ange – how good Celtic were and how great Ange is as a manager; it's well deserved and absolutely true. But there was heartache in that process to become Ange Postecoglou, Celtic manager. That's taking on the best at their own game, going head-to-head against the very best teams with the Australian national team, like World Cup games – they were hectic. We didn't win a game at a World Cup [in 2014], but we were close against Chile and Holland. There's heartache from that.

'I remember a Confederations Cup game against Chile [in 2017], and again we didn't get through to the next round after a 1–1 draw; he was devastated. That determination and motivation to be at his best and be the best manager possible and get on that world stage, he had that taken away from him.'

Coming close and falling just short might have caused some to reconsider their approach. But this is a coach, remember, who followed up that first exit from Football Australia by heading into Greek lower league football and then the semi-pro delights of the Whittlesea Zebras back home in the Melbourne suburbs. He's not easily put off.

There's no surprise, then, that he's been consistent in his messaging during his time in the UK, saying of his approach: 'Where others are chasing just the win, I'm chasing more than that. I'm chasing winning in a certain way. There is no coach in the game who doesn't want to win. But there has to be more than that to drive you.

'It's no different from anywhere else. I'm not happy if we're not winning. From our perspective, there's a clear understanding – we need to get results. We need to win games of football. But I don't want to win games by accident or with a stroke of luck. I don't think that fills belief.

'And I don't like that word momentum because it suggests we're just rolling up and doing stuff. The boys are working awfully hard. There is no sense of them getting comfortable at any stage.'

It's fair to say that 'comfortable' isn't a word that features often in discussions about Postecoglou's management techniques. Yet the confidence he creates within the group makes all the discomfort worthwhile. And players, after all, just want certainty and consistency. If the boss never lets his standards drop, at least they know what to expect.

The same goes for supporters. Up to a point, anyway. With another big European challenge on the horizon, Celtic fans rather hoped that the gaffer would hang around to demonstrate the promised year-on-year improvement against clubs trousering tens of millions from UEFA's central pot on an annual basis. That hope was accompanied by a constant concern that he might move on to more lucrative pastures. Cue the flurry of jokes from ex-Rangers players volunteering to drive Ange to Elland Road, Anfield . . . or maybe even Tottenham Hotspur Stadium.

Cklamovski, as close to Postecoglou as just about anyone in football, knows that his old boss still craves opportunities to prove himself, saying: 'In Yokohama, I had some big, deep and meaningful chats with him. What's his next step?

'He missed out on a few opportunities abroad and it really shattered him. That's part of the heartache that's part of him, and he was blessed to be at a special club like Celtic. He uses that heartache to produce who he is and to make an impact at such a special football club; it's like synergy. I just couldn't have picked a better club for him, with the way they play and their history, Celtic Football Club. It was meant to be. Destined. Destiny.'

Chapter 4

A BOSS IS BORN

THOSE who were actually on board the team bus heading to Sydney Airport on the night in question remember it as a blistering evisceration that made no allowances for old friendships; the fact that he'd shared a pitch, a dressing room and the occasional raucous players' night out with some in his target audience did nothing, absolutely nothing, to temper Ange Postecoglou's fury. Was this the night when a young assistant coach found his managerial voice? Quite possibly. Even if he still had a long way to go, and a lot of influential people to win over, before he'd even be considered alongside some of the big-name candidates being pursued and wooed by the South Melbourne board. Just getting on the shortlist to replace Frank Arok, already doomed by one of those results guaranteed to get any manager the sack, would require a fair bit of schmoozing. Including – and here we must issue a trigger warning for anyone affected by excessive use of national stereotypes – a memorable job pitch delivered to a group of directors gathered around a barbecue. Australia, man. Don't ever change.

Yet it is certainly possible to trace Postecoglou's development as a coach back to the final night of former Socceroo head coach Arok's reign as South gaffer. And an address to the troops that left no one in any doubt over exactly what he would expect from his charges, should he ever be promoted to a position of real power at the club he'd joined as a nipper. Kudos to the bus driver who dutifully handed over the microphone, then, when Postecoglou marched to the front of the team coach and demanded an opportunity to have a few words following South's miserable 3–0 away loss to Marconi-Fairfield Stallions in April 1996. The poor guy might have been cleaning blood, tears and sweat, among other bodily fluids, out of the upholstery for weeks, given the ferocity of what happened next. Let history record that his sacrifice was not in vain.

Peter Filopoulos, who was general manager of South at the time, still recalls all the details of Postecoglou being handed the manager's job – for just three weeks as the most temporary of interims, initially – at a time when one of the biggest clubs in Australia was going through a very real crisis. In particular, Filopoulos remembers the key pieces of oratory that put Ange in a position to prove himself. Starting with a brutal outburst born of fury and frustration on behalf of a good man let down.

Postecoglou had been, in many ways, the ideal number two for Arok. Still close to a lot of senior figures in the dressing room, he could act as a bridge between manager and players. After finishing sixth in Arok's first season, however, the team were struggling badly with just a few weeks of the campaign remaining, as their hopes of making the end-of-season play-offs drifted further and further out of reach.

'And this is a proud club, South Melbourne,' explained Filopoulos. 'The fans, the board, they didn't tolerate failure.

So, with three weeks to go, they decided to let Frank go. But what led to his actual departure was the fourth last game, when we had to go to Marconi, in Sydney. We had to win. And we lost three–nil. And so Frank left.

'But after the game, we were on a bus for a one-hour drive to the airport for our flight back to Melbourne. The players were being jovial, they were mucking around, they were being a bit out of control. Frank got on the coach, slumped in his chair, and was very despondent – and Ange was quite disgusted. And I could see him being agitated when he got up from his seat. He went to the front of the bus and said to the bus driver: "Give me the microphone. Give me the microphone." So he's picked up the microphone, has turned it on. He goes: "I want your attention." They wouldn't shut up. So he shouts: "Shut up and listen! I've played for this club. I want to tell you a few things. I've played for this club from the age of under-8s; I have represented every age group; I've won championships in juniors; I've captained this club to two championships; I'm now assistant coach. I've seen teams right across the board, from under-8s right up. No team I've ever been associated with at this club has ever disgraced the jersey as much as you blokes did tonight."

'Then he picked on one particular player, who must have been laughing or smiling, saying: "If you think it's funny, I want to see how you go next week in the youth team, because that's where you're gonna go next week." So it was one of those unbelievable surprises. And there was dead silence for the rest of the trip. And we got to the airport, and back then it was physical boarding passes, and the players were shuffling boarding passes to make sure no one sat next to Ange.

'Not that I'm a visionary, right, but I remember thinking: "This guy's got something special. I really mean that, he's got something special." We went back and we had a board meeting about Frank that night and reached the unanimous decision to let him go, three games to go, then moved on to discussion about who's going to be the interim coach. I relayed what Ange had done and said on the bus. And it was unanimous. Let's give him an opportunity for the next three games, but let's not think about long-term coaches for now.'

The following morning, the board were ready to announce both the departure of Arok and, as one of those footnotes inevitably included in all such over-capitalised Club Statements, the fact that Ange Postecoglou would be taking charge of the Team for the remaining three fixtures of the season, while the Club searched for a new Manager etc., etc. Just one problem. In an era when we weren't all permanently attached to our mobile phones, they needed to check that the number two was willing to step into the vacancy, even if it was only for a few weeks. Postecoglou was still working in a bank at this stage, cashing cheques and making change for customers while wondering whether he'd ever get a full-time gig with a fully professional club.

Picture the scene, then, as the South Melbourne general manager joined the queue at Ange's station, patiently waiting his turn before approaching the counter and asking when he might be free for a chat outside. Even in a sport which has seen managers tapped up on superyachts, hired in bars of varying repute and sacked in showers or binned in car parks, lining up to ask the bank teller if he fancies taking over as head coach seems a little quirky. True to form, though, the unflappable Ange didn't even blink when informed of the change in circumstances. He simply told Filopoulos to call a meeting of the entire squad – no excuses, no late arrivals – for 6 p.m. Then went back inside to get on with the day job. While planning another key speech, described by the GM as one of the best he's ever heard.

Taking up the story as we sit in an almost empty hotel bar not far from Melbourne Cricket Ground, slapping his hand down on the flat surface for emphasis at points, Filopoulos said: 'I remember clearly what Ange told them: "I've obviously been appointed for the next three games. I don't know who's gonna be the coach long term. But I'll tell you this, coaches don't sack themselves. Because the coach might have made mistakes. But all of you, individually and collectively, have contributed to where we were at the moment as a football club. And you've all contributed to, obviously, the demise of our coach. I'm here for the next three games, and this is the way I want to approach our games for the next three games, all right?" Then, he outlined his manifesto. All the boys walked out. We won the next three games.'

Let the record show that South did, indeed, win the final three fixtures of their 1995–96 season, beating West Adelaide Hellas at home, Brisbane Strikers away and then rounding off with a win over Newcastle Breakers – already vanquished in the Australian Cup Final in January 1996 – back in Melbourne. Postecoglou had earned the gratitude of many. But hadn't exactly put himself in pole position to become manager of such a prestigious club, Filopoulos pointing out: 'We're talking about South Melbourne. The Celtic of Australia. The boardroom discussion about the permanent coach when we finished the season, everyone's talking about the highest profile coach they could find.'

Part of the problem, for Postecoglou, lay in the fact that the South board was just so damned unwieldy at the time. There were the old-timers who ran things, effectively. And a group of younger directors who were more open to new ideas. Possibly the one thing they all agreed on, in fact, was the need for a high-profile manager. Someone with a bit of box-office appeal. Ange didn't even feature in their thinking.

Those closest to him recognised that he had ambitions, of course. They'd watched him struggle to accept that his playing days were over, then throw himself into coaching with a passion, reading everything he could about the great Liverpool boss Bill Shankly, in particular, and delving deeply into how the most successful leaders coped with failure. He took up every opportunity he could to get out on the training pitch, agreeing to run a soccer programme at the prestigious Melbourne Grammar School – and pointing out to South that he was getting more to coach kids than they were giving him in his role as assistant manager with one of the most important clubs in the country. There was an acknowledgement, among South leadership, that he might prove a long-term option. But at the age of 30? With no experience as a manager?

Nicholas Maikousis, the current South president, shrugged his shoulders as he recalled directors deciding to take a punt – eventually – on the kid with Hellas in his heart and a headful of ideas, saying: 'You can't be too sophisticated about coaching appointments and those sorts of decisions. South boy, passionate, always tended to be a leader anyway, a past captain of ours, and he wanted it badly. I don't think it's much more sophisticated than that. It wasn't. You must remember he was unproven. This was his first big club, and remember at the time, it was the biggest club. So, it was a bit of a gamble as well, but it was probably the best decision the club has made for a long, long time. He took over and built something very, very special for us.

'He had probably half a dozen friends, young friends, on the board. But the board was still very much run by a few old-timers. And they were after Zoran Matić, who was with Adelaide City, which was really Adelaide Juventus. He was going to cost a fortune as well. And the young board members didn't want him. So somehow, with negotiations not going well with Zoran Matić, Ange got the job.'

There was a bit more to it than that, obviously. Machinations and negotiations. Winning hearts and minds. Just getting himself considered as an actual contender, in the first place. That wasn't easy. Not when all the talk around South was about bringing in another international candidate or, as most remember it, making a major play for Matić, who had already guided Adelaide to three titles in less than a decade at the helm.

Delving into the memory banks for a story to explain just how far out of the picture Postecoglou was, when all of these other names were being bandied about, former GM Filopoulos said: 'Ange came into my office one day. And, I admired and respected Angie a lot, but this shows what our thinking was. He says to me: "What's going on with the coaching position, big fella?" I naively – I was 24, 25, in my defence – responded with: "Oh, they're talking about X, they're talking about this guy. They're talking about . . ." I can laugh about it now. Not thinking that Ange wouldn't even be remotely interested in knowing about these other guys. Anyway, he goes: "Big fella, what if I'm interested? Has my name come up?" He walked out of the meeting, and I thought, "Fuck. He's right." And I didn't even think about this guy.'

Creeping into the consciousness of a young general manager who considered him a friend was one thing. Getting the board to view him as even a long-shot outsider would take a bit of effort. Including an impromptu job pitch delivered while – another warning here – the fellas were throwing another shrimp on the barbie . . .

Filopoulos revealed: 'I had this idea overnight: "I'm gonna invite him over to my place with a bunch of young board members." There were the older board members and the younger. And the younger board members had the balance of power – but they never really executed anything with their balance of power. So, I invited the young board members and their wives to my place for a barbecue.

'At some stage, what used to happen at these barbecues, the girls would end up inside and the guys would end up outside. I said to Ange: "When we break out into one of those, maybe you should plead your case to the young board members, unsolicited, and see how they respond. Maybe it's a little bit of you building your own narrative, Ange."

'So that's how it panned out. Conversation started about the coach of South Melbourne and all the young board members are saying: "Yeah, now what about Zoran Matić? We're talking to . . ." and then someone asks Ange what he thinks. They ask him who he would go for. He just goes: "Well, they're all good names. But I think I can do the job. And this is how I would do the job. And this is what I will do." He went on for about 30 minutes. I remember the vice president at the time turns around and says: "Ange, you're our next coach!" '

Cue more laughter from Filopoulos, the experienced sports administrator and executive genuinely tickled by the memory of a young Ange just blowing away his audience with passion, knowledge and a vision. The more time you spend talking to people who have worked alongside Postecoglou, the easier it is to imagine him holding an audience – players, fellow coaches, directors or supporters – in the palm of his hand by force of character and clarity of message. In this instance, the younger board members went to work, persuading their fellow directors that promoting the former captain would solve many of the problems that kept South from realising their full potential. He certainly wasn't going to be found wanting when it came to effort or commitment.

Speak to the guys who worked with him during his four years as South boss, and they'll all drop one word into the conversation at some point: relentless. He demanded a great deal from his players. And he forced his superiors to try harder, just to keep up. A 17-hour working day wasn't that unusual as he looked to revolutionise virtually every aspect of the football department, basing his expectations on the methodology used – and standards set – at the biggest professional clubs on the planet. Why couldn't South borrow ideas and ideals from Bayern Munich or Real Madrid? If they might never have the money of a Manchester

United or Barcelona, it cost nothing to steal some of the policies that kept those clubs competing at the top end year after year.

If players were expected to be more professional in every aspect of their daily lives, with the introduction of a code of conduct setting high standards, they would also be given a more valued status within the organisation. For instance, where once just about anyone could wander in and out of the first-team dressing room, now it was to become a sanctuary for players; any 'outsider' seeking entry had to knock first and wait to be invited. Little changes like that made a big difference. It suggests that, even as a managerial rookie, Postecoglou knew that he had to take people along with him. He couldn't just stand up at the front of the room and bark out demands. He understood the value of having everyone – players, the kit man, the general manager and everyone in the boardroom – buy into his reasons for effecting a total revolution in attitude and ambition. In something of a recurring theme during his career, those players who didn't commit wholeheartedly were quietly shown the door, replaced by the sorts of characters more amenable to the manager's philosophy.

The only problem for Postecoglou? Not even the most powerful gaffer can get rid of board members prone to questioning their methods. When his changes failed to produce instant results at the start of the 1996–97 season, there were plenty in the boardroom itching to make a quick change. He was certainly under pressure after winning just once in the opening seven rounds of league fixtures, with three losses and three draws causing rumblings of discontent in the directors' box, Filopoulos admitting: 'There were some people on the board – who were on the wrong side – who never believed in Ange.'

Heading into round eight, the boardroom agitators looking for an excuse to axe the manager were rubbing their hands in anticipation. Even amongst his supporters on the board, there was unrest over Postecoglou's vision – sold to them with such conviction – failing to produce results. The fact that their next match was away to Marconi-Fairfield, a replay of the fixture that had ultimately left Arok in an untenable position, added an extra air of doom to the situation, Filopoulos adamantly declaring: 'If he hadn't won, he was gone. That's a fact, he was gone.

'But we won. We won one–nil with a goal from his best mate, Paul Trimboli. He scored a scrappy goal – those guys are inseparable, by the way – in the 89th minute [the records show his goal came after 87 minutes, but we'll forgive a little artistic licence in the retelling of a great story]. And the rest is history. That moment for me, I look back at that moment and think that could have been the end of Ange Postecoglou's career.'

In all honesty, everything Postecoglou has achieved in the game since – despite suffering some pretty major setbacks – suggests he wouldn't have been put off, had his first crack at management been strangled at birth. He would have found another opening, worked his way back to the top. Just not with South Melbourne, who probably wouldn't have won back-to-back titles and, of course, the Oceania Championship that secured them passage to the 2000 FIFA World Club Championship in Brazil. There would be no Ange Postecoglou Field – home training venue for the South junior sides – in Middle Park. Fortunately for all involved, Trimboli's goal steadied the ship, results turned around and even the doubters on the board had to admit that reaching the preliminary finals – the first stages of the Aussie play-off system – represented a decent effort for someone in their first season of management, leading a team bearing no resemblance to the no-hopers of the previous year's campaign.

Not that Postecoglou was satisfied with that, of course. He continued to cajole and demand, persuade and direct, forcing everyone to work harder, making it his daily duty to challenge individuals and push them to new heights. And yes, there was a touch of 'my way or the highway' about his approach. But only up to a point. People who were in the building at the time testify that Carl Halford, his assistant coach, was much more than just a nodding yes-man who put out the cones and gathered up the balls once training was finished. There would be regular consultations between them, with Postecoglou open to taking on ideas.

On the field, the onus shifted even further towards overwhelming opponents with swarming attacks. The philosophy that would underpin every stage of Postecoglou's development as a coach was clear, even then. Training sessions were about the ball moving quickly, criss-crossing the field to drag opponents out of position and exploiting the spaces created.

His sessions were uptempo and high quality, with an emphasis on honing phases of play guaranteed to produce chances. They didn't always come off on game day. But he gave his team as many opportunities as possible to break down defences. He was really beginning to enjoy the technical and tactical side of the job, taking pride in seeing his plans and schemes carried out successfully – and thrilling to the sight of players develop and improve under his guidance. Those things gave him more joy than the back-to-back championship triumphs. Although he will admit that those Grand Final victories, over Carlton Soccer Club in 1998 and Sydney United the following year, were pretty sweet.

Before he was done with his involvement in South Melbourne, he'd add a famous triumph in Fiji and lead them to the Maracanã Stadium, where 85,000 Vasco da Gama fans lay in wait. By the time he left to take up a job as coach of the Australian youth sides, South had established themselves as a dominant force in both the country and the Oceania region.

Maikousis, leaning back in his chair and contemplating the shifting fates that saw South and all the other 'ethnic' clubs cleansed from Australia's national stage as the new A-League franchises were parachuted into prime markets, admitted: 'This club has been in the dark ages for the last 20 years. And yet, our brand is still recognised as one of excellence. We still have significant support 20 years later. And remember we haven't been in the top flight of Australian football for all of that time. But the fact that we are where we are, still going strong, still recognised and looking to return to the national stage? That has a lot to do with the period of success we had with Ange.'

Nobody ever makes all the right decisions for all the right reasons. And even the most successful will admit to their achievements relying on a degree of dumb luck, to some extent. But the smartest do have a habit of knowing when to keep their head down. And when to speak up. On that miserable coach journey from Bossley Park to the Sydney airport, Postecoglou could have stayed in his seat and quietly stewed over the attitude of players who had failed his gaffer, his team, his club. It would have been easy, perhaps, to keep shtum and let the cards fall as they may. Knowing that Arok was probably for the chop, some in his position might even have gone out of their way to curry favour with senior players, with a view to presenting themselves as a natural successor. Ange made a very different choice. He took a stand. And demonstrated the very qualities that would, one day, after many more triumphs and setbacks, great leaps forward and wrong-footed stumbling down dead ends, enable him to become a truly trailblazing pioneer for Australian coaching.

Key Game

MARCONI-FAIRFIELD 0 SOUTH MELBOURNE 1

30 November 1996

SEVEN games into National Soccer League season 1996–97 and Ange Postecoglou, promoted from assistant manager to caretaker and then from interim to 'permanent' gaffer, was already under enormous pressure. South had only won one league game. According to those who were on the scene at the time, even some within the club were wondering whether they'd made a mistake in appointing such a young and inexperienced coach – regardless of his status as a great club captain – to a job that carried enormous responsibility and scrutiny.

They were just three points off the foot of the table. And now they were heading back to Fairfield, to the very stadium where sacked predecessor Frank Arok's fate had been sealed just a few months earlier. A must-win game? You could say that, even if Postecoglou himself has said that he was completely oblivious to the idea that his job might be on the line.

A scrappy goal from best mate Paul Trimboli in the 87th minute was enough to get South this vital win, in round eight of the competition, and quieten some of the chatter surrounding the rookie boss. They'd go on to finish third. Before winning back-to-back titles in 1997–98 and 1998–99. Maybe that would all have happened, regardless. Perhaps, even if South had lost to Fairfield, the board would have held their nerve and stuck with a young man of real vision. Football being as fickle as a feather in a windstorm, though, failure to win may well have cut short Ange Postecoglou's first crack at management.

Chapter 5

TAKING ON THE WORLD

A FROG-INFESTED field in Fiji and being showered with cups of Brazilian piss. Neither scenario is likely to be covered in any coaching manual. But any manager trying to make a name for themselves on the global stage surely has to expect a few unpleasant surprises along the way. The fact that Ange Postecoglou came through both situations figuratively, if not literally, smelling of roses, perhaps explains why he often seems so unflappable in the face of each new 'crisis' to have confronted him since his move to Europe. You think this is stressful? Oh, mate, have I got a story to tell you . . .

Postecoglou's coaching career hit the stratosphere, at least in Australian terms, when he followed up back-to-back Grand Final wins with South Melbourne by leading his boyhood club to glory in the 1999 Oceania Club Championship, hosted in the Fijian towns of Nadi and Lautoka. Victory in that tournament, which saw South vie for regional supremacy alongside the champions of New Zealand, Samoa, American Samoa, Solomon Islands, Tahiti, Tonga, Vanuatu and the host nation, would deliver the opportunity of a lifetime. An invitation to compete in the inaugural FIFA World Club Championship in January

2000. You may remember it for many different reasons. Possibly top of the list would be the massive controversy surrounding Manchester United being allowed to drop out of the FA Cup in order to take part in Brazil; there were questions in the House, protests in the stands over the cup holders treating the world's oldest knockout competition with utter disdain, accusations suggesting all sorts of interference by politicians eager to garner support for England's bid to host the 2006 World Cup. How did that work out, again?

Those of us lucky to be in Rio and São Paulo covering the tournament recall plenty of arguments and even the odd scandal. Treble winners United were in a foul humour from the moment they set foot on Brazilian soil, the famously grumpy Sir Alex Ferguson setting the tone by shutting the world's media out from all but the most strictly mandated press conferences. That left us to look elsewhere for stories. In some cases, that meant gleefully reporting the words of any Brazilian legend willing to have a pop at the arrogant English visitors; the local greats seemed to have a particular penchant for picking on David Beckham, if memory serves. For the few of us allowed to find relief on the opposition beat, of course, there were always alternative interview opportunities. Like whassisname. The boss of that Aussie outfit. Ange something or other. He seems up for it. Confident enough, too, isn't he?

Right about here is where you'd expect the author to wax lyrical about that chat enjoyed with Postecoglou in a media suite overlooking Ipanema Beach, the anecdote ending with something along the lines of: 'And you know what? There was something about that guy . . .' Apologies for not playing along. But I genuinely can't remember what he said, the questions we asked or, to be frank, anything about the young South Melbourne boss. They weren't the story. And were expected to provide very little in the way of opposition to the established teams.

Drawn alongside Champions League winners United, CONCACAF champions Necaxa, from Mexico, and Copa Libertadores winners Vasco da Gama, South duly finished bottom of Group B. But were generally held to have acquitted themselves well, as a team of part-time footballers required to play three games – all in the famous Estadio Maracanã – over the space of six days. It was an experience, all right. For everyone involved. And it began, before a ball was kicked in anger, with a warm welcome by the Vasco fans. Warm and wet.

Current South president Nicholas Maikousis, then a young director charged with helping the manager navigate the complexities of an entirely new tournament in an alien environment, couldn't help but smile as he recalled: 'I remember we were taken to Flamengo, I think that's where we were training, and we had police escort motorbikes closing down the streets; the bus going straight through. That was extraordinary. I think that was probably the biggest thing, coming from a country like Australia – where, you know, football was not the number one sport, and is not the number one sport now – to go to a place like that where they're urinating on you from the stands, and you need umbrellas to get off the team bus. Yeah, they put it in cups and threw it. The abuse we copped just trying to get the bus around was extraordinary. In terms of our favourite games, we all have our personal choices. The first Grand Final we won under Ange was, for me, very special. But the Vasco da Gama game was enormous. Even with the cups of piss. It was enormous.'

Being honest, here, Nicholas. That doesn't sound like a great lark. More like torture. Or at least a tactic designed to intimidate anyone venturing on to Vasco's turf. As if the team they had at the time, including a strike force of Edmundo and Romario, wasn't scary enough.

To say that South were like babes in the wood at this global tournament would be exaggerating things just a little. But it certainly took the well-meaning amateurs in charge of the travelling party a few days to get to grips with the chaotic nature of South American scheduling. Especially in a tournament that honestly felt as if organisers were making it up as they went along. Nothing was ever set in stone, with timetables considered mere guidelines and late changes to plans treated as an inevitable occurrence. Just keeping track of where everyone was – as opposed to where they were supposed to be, according to the schedule, hand-book or latest official update – was a struggle.

Maikousis enjoys telling a story intended to underline his own difficulties in getting to grips with the distinctly Brazilian approach to organisation, laughing at the collect-ive naivety of the boys from Prahran, South Yarra, Richmond and surrounding neighbourhoods suddenly transported to an alien environment as he said: 'Our first experience with Vasco ... now that was something. We were training in Flamengo, and all the journalists were coming to us because they didn't have access to the other big teams, particularly Man U. So I had Peter, the FIFA media liaison officer, with me the whole time. Anyway, on this day, he said: "You're going, obviously, to watch Vasco tonight; they've got a practice match on – a friendly." I said: "Of course we are, Peter . . . now excuse me for one moment." I ran across to Ange and said: "We're going to a practice game tonight." We had no idea.

'They were playing the Algerian Olympic team, from memory. FIFA had given us this chauffeur-driven car for the tournament. So we went. Ange, myself and a couple of the other board members. There were 30–40,000 people at this practice game.

'I'm thinking about what we're going to see and yes, you dream that our game against Vasco could go either way. Well, they rip the Algerian Olympic team to shreds. Because that Vasco team I think had six or seven either current or former Brazilian internationals. And I genuinely thought this could be really embarrassing for us. Honestly, that was what I was thinking that night. But we turned up, right?'

The South Melbourne party did talk about expectations with the manager ahead of the tournament, with most expecting Postecoglou to prioritise the Necaxa match – the middle game, sandwiched between that opener against Vasco and the crack at United – in terms of looking for a result. In the end, he went for the win against the Brazilians, fielding his strongest side in a 2–0 loss. Then took the same approach against the Mexicans, losing 3–1, before his leg-weary lads lost to Ferguson's Treble winners by two goals to nil. There was no way Ange was going to send his team out to shut up shop and hope for a draw in any of the games. It never was his style. When his old colleagues saw Celtic going out to have a bash at Real Madrid in the Santiago Bernabéu, well, they just shook their heads and said: 'Yep, that's our Angie.'

There had been a generally accepted view that South Melbourne didn't really belong in such company. That a country unable to sustain a full-time professional league had no business being represented in a tournament intended to celebrate excellence. A few may well have feared some embarrassing scorelines, given the gulf in quality between the best and worst teams in the tournament. But Postecoglou fostered a belief, among his players and his superiors, that South deserved to be mixing with such exalted company. And, as a coach, he craved the opportunity to pit his wits against a true legend like Ferguson, in particular.

The manager gave short shrift to anyone who dared suggest, ahead of the draw for the finals, that they should be hoping to avoid Fergie's all-conquering United. Plenty around South were willing to say as much, in private. But the manager took an entirely different view. He flew to Brazil hoping to be pitted against the very best – and praying that he'd get the chance to lead his team out at the Maracanã. This was many years before the dusty old cauldron was refurbished for the 2014 World Cup, which meant it wasn't exactly the sort of modern arena to which the European players, in particular, had become accustomed. But, man, the history of the place. You could feel it in every crack in the terracing, every step climbed to reach your seat. For anyone of Postecoglou's generation, too young to have seen the greatest Brazil team of all time but raised on tales of Pelé, Gerson, Rivellino et al., the thrill of being at the spiritual home of these legends – the place where crowds of over 100,000 were once commonplace – more than compensated for any lack of creature comforts.

In the middle of all this – the chaos and the beauty of Brazilian crowds gathering two hours before kick-off, the sight of Edmundo torturing defenders just because he could, the whole mix of colour, noise and spectacular talent that made for a memorable event – Postecoglou had to maintain some sort of equilibrium. And find a way to manage the emotions of his players. A word here. A sentence there. A simple plan that gave them a chance, he felt, of turning Australian football's best face to the watching – or half watching, anyway – world.

'Looking back, it was a lot of fun,' said Maikousis. 'But from a club perspective, it was uncharted territory for us. A lot of the foreign journos prior to the tournament, they were taking the piss because you know, I think our striker J.A. [John Anastasiadis] owned a service station, a petrol station, just up the road here. They had him as a fuel pump attendant, playing against the great Man United. But Ange had a great group of boys around him. They did us proud, every one of them.

'I just think Ange had a really different perspective. He sees games against the biggest teams as a massive opportunity. We had a lot of good players, almost virtually all Australian-born, but the problem was the speed of the closing down and the tackling, all that sort of stuff when you're semi-pro. So, I think he always knew that he was gonna have a challenge. But he wasn't going to shy away from it. He wanted to take them on.'

South had already achieved their ultimate goal just in qualifying for the inaugural FIFA tournament, courtesy of winning an Oceania Championship event that could hardly have been more low-key, in terms of prestige, opposition . . .

or facilities. Fiji, a rugby country to the exclusion of almost all other sports, was chosen as the host nation for the nine-club championship, which would see teams split into groups of three, with the winners of each section joining the best second-placed finisher in the semi-finals. After coming from behind to beat Solomon Islands champions Malaita Eagles, the Aussies battered a misfiring Konica Machine, of America Samoa, 10–0 to reach the last four. Tahiti Ligue 1 champs Vénus were beaten 3-0 in the semi-final, setting up an all-or-nothing finale against Fijian favourites Nadi, who would have home field advantage at Prince Charles Park.

Witnesses to Postecoglou's preparations for this tournament, which might have been taken lightly by a few in the travelling party, testify to the fact that he spent long hours preparing the perfect game plan for each test; he could often be found mulling over some hypothetical problem when virtually everyone else was fast asleep. Nothing he dreamt up, however, could have compared to the actual scenes that greeted South when they arrived for the final.

'The pitch was full of frogs,' said Maikousis, laughing at the memory of a truly surreal sight. 'Frogs. Yeah. So, we've gone from Fiji, one extreme, to the Maracanã. The Oceania Championship, it was good fun. But it was played in a real backwater, compared to us.

'I remember we were actually losing the first game, which was a shock. We ended up winning late, 2–1. And that's a game changer. I mean, first of all, we actually got US$3.8 million from qualifying for Brazil. Remember I said there were still a couple of old-timers on the board? The president at the time was running up and down the touchline.

That's a true story, during the game. We were losing. Having said that, though, I don't think we actually knew the total financial position. I think we had heard your 700, 800,000. Then, when it became $3.8 million, that was a bit of a game changer. It's probably just as well that the president didn't know the real numbers when he was running up and down the touchline.

'I think we've all got some pretty special memories of that tournament, though. The whole resort was probably 50 years old. We had one breakout room or entertaining room – and all I remember is dancing to ABBA's "Dancing Queen". It was on their jukebox because that's what it was then; we didn't have iPhones.'

They could dance. They could jive. Having the time of their lives. And why not? They'd taken a giant leap for not just their own club, but Australian football as a whole. With a bunch of part-time footballers, led by a coach who had only just turned 34 years of age. Most importantly, they had earned themselves a chance to take on the world. In a country where football is the be-all and end-all, the here, the now and the everlasting. Nothing that happened now could possibly rain on their parade. Even if they would have been advised to pack brollies, raincoats and galoshes for that first trip to the Maracanã.

Key Game

CELTIC 0 REAL MADRID 3

Celtic Park, Glasgow
Tuesday, 6 September 2022

FOR the little boy who used to get up in the middle of the Melbourne night to watch big European games, this was the stuff of dreams. Or, rather, the culmination of a lifelong ambition. One rooted in precious bonding moments with his father.

Seeing the famously stern and taciturn Jim Postecoglou come alive with excitement in the wee small hours, feeling like they were the only two people awake in the entire country, young Ange wanted to be part of something with such a powerful transformative effect. However long it took, whatever hurdles had to be cleared, he would get there. One day.

And, although nothing in the world could ever shift his boyhood allegiance to the great Liverpool side of the 1970s, his stint as South Melbourne captain under the management of Real legend Ferenc Puskás definitely left him with a special feeling for Los Blancos. When his first crack at the Champions League saw Celtic drawn against the holders, who would visit Glasgow on Matchday 1 of Group F, well, it seemed like fate.

Although Celtic lost, this might have been one of their best performances under Postecoglou, who was without a couple of key players – yet still saw his team squander three good chances in a thrilling expression of attacking football.

The fact that Real eventually made their quality show was, in the end, inevitable. But not the point.

Singling out this game as a special memory, Postecoglou said: 'Real Madrid are there in their white kits, Carlo Ancelotti is in the opposite technical area and I'm managing Celtic. And I knew that, if I wasn't there, I would have been getting up in the middle of the night to watch that game. Yet here I was, smack-dab in the middle of it. Now, at my age, I took a minute to appreciate it.

'The fans at Celtic know football. Obviously, they're one-eyed about their team but, when Luka Modrić comes off, they're still applauding him because they recognise a great player. We lose 3–0 and they're still applauding because they've seen a great game.

'When I first got the job, a lot of people who knew Celtic, or people who had worked at the top level of the game, reached out to say: "Look, Celtic Park on European nights is special; no matter what you've experienced, you won't have seen anything like this." Being there that night, I understood.'

Chapter 6

WANDERING IN THE WILDERNESS

IF you've heard about the famous mural on the wall of Nunawading FC's modest little clubhouse, an unimposing structure tucked in behind the Tally Ho Scout Troop hall in a green and pleasant suburb of Greater Melbourne, you'll have a fair idea of the esteem in which Ange Postecoglou is held by fans of this proper community club. It's safe to say they're definitely admirers of the man now immortalised alongside two of the most influential coaches in the history of football: Johan Cruyff and Pep Guardiola.

The story behind the painting – a much misunderstood gesture, insists the man who commissioned it – is every bit as intriguing as the work itself. Because it speaks to the enthusiasm that kept Postecoglou plugging away at football during the most infuriating period of his career. The quality and dedication he brought to everything he did. His refusal to consider himself too good, too important, or too advanced to work with 11-year-olds. At a time when he wondered if the game had given up on him.

Rewind to his departure as Young Socceroos coach in 2007 and you'll find a turning point in the life and career of a man who might have been broken by the experience.

That he didn't simply take a break from the game, after a quarter of a century as a player and then coach, is testament to something far greater than mere enthusiasm. Because the two years that followed saw Ange – multiple title winner, forward-thinking tactician and future visionary destined to become one of Australia's most admired sporting exports – throw himself headlong into a couple of misadventures that certainly add colour to his backstory.

There was the brief stint taking charge of a team in the Greek lower leagues, answering a call from the old country in the hope of an enriching life experience. Yeah, well, that ended with him dashing to the airport with his pocket stuffed full of euros – money he was owed after going without pay for four months. Or the rare experience of relegation with a local team back in Melbourne; his stint helping out Victoria Premier League side Whittlesea Zebras does not feature prominently in any history of a manager with so many successes on his CV. Nor do many focus much on the work he did at Nunawading, a community club who were delighted when Postecoglou agreed to set up a youth programme based on principles familiar to anyone who has seen Ange-ball in action.

Virtually everyone interviewed for this book was eager to mention the time Postecoglou spent away from elite football, toiling away under a cloud following an infamous televised interview with player-turned-pundit Craig Foster. If you haven't seen it, that's what YouTube is for. In a nutshell, Foster rips an increasingly tetchy Ange limb from limb, metaphorically speaking, over his team's failure to qualify for the FIFA Youth World Cup Finals. Think of it as a bit like the famous televised showdown between Brian

Clough and Don Revie from 1974. Only with more enmity and animosity. Postecoglou, already pretty much guaranteed to leave his post anyway, bristled at Foster's increasingly hostile attempts to force some admission – of responsibility, culpability, even guilt – from him.

It was not his finest hour and, when he speaks about it now, he freely admits that the stink caused by such a frank exchange of views made it extremely tough to find another job in Australian football, even revealing: 'There was one job I actually got, where the owner hadn't seen the interview. Then he just saw the interview and they pulled out, like: "Nah, we can't have this guy as manager of the football club . . ." I remember straight after doing it, that's all people wanted to talk about, that interview. I thought, "Is that what I'm going to be defined by now?"'

To give you an idea of how brutal it all was, consider the verdict of Georgia Postecoglou, Ange's wife, who admitted: 'For the first time I heard him over the phone really distressed. He was pretty upset and worried about how he was portrayed and what it looked like.'

There is an acceptance, in retrospect, that the governing body didn't do nearly enough to support their coach. He was an easy scapegoat. Someone to blame for institutional failings that left the country's best young footballers desperately short of exposure to competitive first-team football.

Truth be told, he'd also had enough of the parochialism and lack of confidence that always seemed to undermine soccer Down Under. Whoever thought there would be such a thing as an Aussie cringe, right? Whatever you want to call it, Ange was fed up with the mealy-mouthed approach taken by the federation. He needed a change of scene. But he'd just made his search for new horizons unnecessarily awkward.

While killing time working as an 'elite consultant' for Football Federation Victoria and exploring the world of punditry, the chance arose to embrace what he now calls 'the chaos of Greek football' when Australian-based businessman Con Makris invited Ange to take charge of boyhood heroes Panachaiki FC, a proud club from the one-team city of Patras, a team who had fallen on hard times in more ways than one. If it wasn't quite the life-changing European opportunity always envisaged by a young Postecoglou dreaming of making the big time, the fact that Panachaiki were aiming for promotion to Super League 2 carried a certain attraction. As did the opportunity to go 'home', improve his grasp of the Greek language and immerse himself in a culture that had been such a significant part of his immigrant life in Australia.

Postecoglou himself talks with real affection about the brief time he spent at Panachaiki – he was gone by December of the same year – and the lessons he learned there. If having his team selections picked apart by the local priest was a novelty, the standard of football was good enough for Ange to try out some ideas that he still uses to this day. While he makes no bones about the fact that only being virtually unemployable in Australia prompted him to leap at the Greek offer, he doesn't regret it. Especially as he got out at just the right moment. Without suffering the sort of financial hit that tends to be accepted as an acceptable risk for those working in an always-volatile environment.

Long-time assistant Peter Cklamovski, who followed his gaffer to Patras, claims good memories from their time in

Greece far outweigh the bad, although he concedes that his opinion is probably influenced by Ange's clever exit strategy when a change of ownership – midway through their first proper season at the helm – left the management team with another big decision to make. Had Postecoglou not managed to negotiate a full settlement of all money due, never a guarantee in Greek football, he might not look back on that period with quite the same degree of fondness.

'It was an amazing chapter; I really enjoyed it,' said Cklamovski. 'It was our first taste of football in Europe. A proud club and an amazing little experience, although it ended prematurely due to an ownership change mid-season, which I think took everybody by surprise, even all of Greece by surprise as well. We were top of the table at the time – first or second but certainly very close, we were right up there. We were talking about promotion – that was legitimately our ambition. Get promoted and keep going; we did have a long-term view there.

'But, as that chapter progressed, there was a short period of time when staff and players weren't getting paid – not just delayed, they weren't getting paid. Maybe three or four months, staff and players weren't getting paid. And that affected a lot of the group; you can imagine Greek society and players live by the day. What I was amazed by was how Ange kept that group together. He can communicate in Greek, so I was trying to learn as much as I could in terms of the Greek language, but how he had everybody on his side and pushing in the same direction – even without getting paid – and still producing great football, a real team mentality and not losing the group, or having any chaos around the group. A genuine leader. It was just amazing to see.'

All of the good vibes in the world could not, however, mask the problems that resulted in Makris selling out to Alexis Kougias, whose takeover – while not completed until early 2009 – was well under way when Postecoglou decided that this might be an opportune moment to cut his losses. But not before putting the squeeze on the new chairman.

Taking up the story, Cklamovski explained: 'The new owner came in halfway through the season, and Ange says to me: "This owner is coming in. Do you want to stay or go?"'

'And I said: "Mate, if you stay, I'll stay. If you go, I'll go. A simple decision because I've got no idea, it's your call."'

'So he says: "Okay, we're going." As it turned out, a good decision because chaos was around the club. We played our last game on a Sunday, and we didn't tell the players until after the game. A few players picked up that we were leaving, and it was a zero–zero game, and then in the last ten minutes we scored two goals – which often happens in Ange's football – so we win 2–0. We go into the changing rooms as winners, then Ange walks into the changing room, shuts the door behind him, and tells the group. Then he goes to a press conference and announces it in the press conference. The new owner turns up, gives another press conference, and the questions were all: "Why is Ange leaving?" And the new owner didn't have a clue about it. It was a real sweet, sharp way to get the job done.'

Laughing when asked to explain what made it such a smart move, Cklamovski said: 'Well, Ange made sure all the players were well looked after – and we made sure to get the money in our pockets. Honestly, away we went with actual euros in our pockets, so it was . . . [laughing again] . . .

Ange made sure of it and that was part of the plan. It was a funny trip back home.'

You can just imagine the scene, can't you? Ange turning his steely stare on the incoming owner and, wisely, refusing to accept a cheque. It's a wonder he didn't frogmarch the poor sap to the nearest bank to collect the thousands of euros he and Cklamovski would be stowing in their hand luggage on the flight back to Australia. He was applying the number one rule of any business. However much you enjoy your work, it's still that. Work. So make sure you get paid. Especially, as was the case in this instance, he didn't have another job to fall back on.

Finding part-time work with Whittlesea Zebras, who as Brunswick Juventus had been one of the many 'ethnic clubs' cleared out to make way for the new A-League franchises, Postecoglou talks about his time with the semi-professional club as valuable experience, describing it alternatively as 'the factory floor' and 'the bottom of the food chain'. It's fair to say they didn't have their problems to seek. The fact that they were relegated was, insist those who were at the club, not down to any lack of ability or commitment by the gaffer.

In the background to all of the above, meanwhile, Postecoglou had begun work on a project much closer to his heart. Inspired by a desire to see young players, his own eldest boy among them, get the right sort of grounding in the game. That's where Nunawading FC enter the story. Or, rather, where Nick Dimitrakis comes barrelling into the tale at hurricane force, scattering goodwill, affection and infectious ambition across the path of anyone venturing out to Forest Hill – a good hour from South Yarra/

Prahran by a combination of tram and old-fashioned shoe leather – to visit the club's home ground of Mahoney's Reserve.

It's a lovely spot, the centrepiece of it all an immaculate grass pitch behind a chain link fence, the presence of smaller goals being stored along the touchlines showing that the club's younger teams are considered every bit as important as their NPL Victoria 3 senior men's side. Not unlike one of the smaller English non-league or Scottish Junior grounds, there's a clubhouse sitting at the top of some steep terracing running along one side of the playing surface and some new-looking floodlights towering over the whole scene. Just across the car park, the club also have a share in a community pavilion with the local cricket club, whose oval boasts one of those old-fashioned manual scoreboards. Another oval is just beyond the trees behind one goal. Walk into the pavilion on a weekday morning and you'll find one of any number of local groups – it's also home to table tennis and badminton, according to the noticeboard pinned outside – making use of the facility. On the day when it was agreed to meet Dimitrakis, popping in to use the loo involved asking directions from an indoor bowls group (no guess is being made at the average age, for fear of causing an offence) rolling up their mats and stacking chairs. Outside, a local authority worker is taking 60 seconds to remove a spray paint 'tag' – the badge of semi-rebellious youth in many a respectable neighbourhood – from a metal junction box. This is suburban life in all its quiet glory.

Which makes the arrival of Dimitrakis – complete with a hale-and-hearty greeting of 'All right, Jonno?! Good to meet ya, mate!' – a very definite change of pace. And this is before he's even started on one of his pet subjects. The impact of Postecoglou on a club with a vision to become a leading light in youth development.

Dimitrakis takes up the story at breakneck speed, explaining: 'One of my closest friends, Greg Mangonis, he was coaching with Ange at a particular V-Elite programme [a Football Federation Victoria initiative] that they had here in Melbourne. The money dried up then, so he, Greg, who's our technical director here, said: "Ange is the man you've been looking for. This type of programme you've been asking me for? Yeah, this is it." And I went to one of those sessions. To be honest, I might have been there for five minutes. The way it was set up and the way there were drills I'd never seen before, I thought this is it. The new evolution of the game, I wasn't part of that, and had no knowledge of it – but I wanted my son to be part of. And then Ange was bringing his own boy, James, to the programme. That was great for us, too.

'I couldn't really believe Ange was just kicking his heels at that time. Because he still had a really strong record from his South Melbourne days. The way he stopped being the coach of the Australian youth side, obviously, was not amicable. So, yes, it was a surprise. And I thought it was an opportunity. And what we had here was that opportunity to use his knowledge and intellectual property to begin a new programme. It was actually an opportunity for me – I didn't care about the noise in the background. It was his intellectual property, and we're gonna have access to it now. Let's make the most of it.

'The kids he worked with were 11 at the time. They were getting stimulated, because there was something different to what they were used to. There were a lot of academies run at the time – and they were probably doing stuff I was doing 25 to 30 years ago. Ange brought in things like the coach always putting balls into play, no waiting time for any kids when we're training for an hour. If a ball went out, the coach has to be ready with another ball straight away. We're talking seconds. In the end, the goal was to have, as a minimum, 1,000 touches per session. That was one of the goals set at the time and that was fascinating. We used it to sell ourselves to parents, like: "Yeah, a thousand touches. You go to another session, and you'll see a lot of lag time. You just focus on any child, and they might only get half of that, so you start to multiply that over years . . ." And maybe that's why this club has had, in the last five years, three players represent Australia at the 17s level. It's why we had Jake Brimmer sign for Liverpool. We have a structured programme and Ange was a big part of that.'

Get into the nuts and bolts of the programme and those who worked with Postecoglou at Nunawading said he was particularly keen to change the way Australian kids used possession, making more use of lateral movements to shift opponents around and create openings. Well aware that each new generation of children seems to have less and less unstructured play time with a ball at their feet, he was determined to prioritise the most important elements in every coaching session. Regardless of the short-term pain involved.

'If anyone went long, he wasn't happy,' said Dimitrakis, with a laugh. 'That's the easy way. He always challenges players. So it's a challenging environment. Especially for parents. There was a lot of education there as well. At the beginning it was really complex, because there wasn't the data to show. Now we can say we've had a few children represent Australia at the 17s level. Now we tell everyone we've had one sign with Liverpool and one got Player of the Year in the A-League. But at the beginning, even myself, I wasn't sure of the direction we were going to end up.

'When Ange has a philosophy, and whatever that encompasses, it's a non-negotiable after that. He'll have the media, he'll have people in the know about the game, and they'll all attack him – like we saw at the beginning of his regime at Celtic. Ange is very strong-minded. And hence, probably why he's successful.

'He keeps an interest in us, too. His son, James, was here for a period of time. So, he was coming and watching a lot of the games. And if we were doing something wrong, he would let us know! He would turn up out of the blue when you least expected. He knew the programme was doing well because he would choose probably the least technical player in a group in one particular month, and then come back later and see that kid. If that child had developed, he knew everyone else had developed. That's how his mind was.'

Nunawading now have around 20 coaches working with teams of all ages, following a blueprint put in place by a man now immortalised in pale blue and black paint. Dimitrakis insists that a lot of pundits, in particular, leapt on the famous mural for all the wrong reasons. The intent was never to put Postecoglou on a par with Cruyff – the most influential thinker in the history of football, quite possibly – or the great man's most successful disciple, Guardiola. Yet he insists: 'All three of those guys think outside of the square. They don't think like other people.

'They understand that the important thing is you need a philosophy. It's probably more important at a development stage versus even at senior level. Ange has got one, Pep's got it. Some might be for and others against it. But that particular philosophy at junior level is very important because it provides a lot of experiences.

'Look, there was massive interest in Celtic here because of Ange. And people here really appreciate the work he's done, can see how good he is. Part of that is something I've noticed with both Ange and Pep, the fact that they've both worked as youth coaches – and their philosophy has translated from youths into seniors. We watched Celtic and saw a lot of the same things Ange was preaching to 11-year-olds here at Nunawading.'

No one at Nunawading is seriously disappointed that Postecoglou didn't get to devote more time to their development, his recruitment by Brisbane Roar in 2009 obviously requiring total commitment. And yielding more success, playing a style of football that the kids back at Mahoney's Reserve would all recognise only too well. The wilderness years were useful, possibly even necessary, for a coach who used his time away from the demands of elite football to develop and reflect, improve – and plan for the next big opportunity. But that's easy to say in retrospect. At the time, being shut out of the business he loved was torture, absolute torture.

Close friend Peter Filopoulos, reflecting on the possibility that his old pal might have been lost to the game forever, makes no effort to sugar-coat the bare facts of Ange's life between leaving his Football Australia post in early 2007 and returning to the big time with Brisbane in October

2009, the former South Melbourne general manager only sounding mildly defensive as he argued: 'Some would say that he didn't do well with the Young Socceroos. I would say that I don't think the Federation at the time provided the right environment or resources for him to succeed. There was the logistical problem. The demise of the National League at the time, as well. The lack of money or lack of investment for him to be able to succeed.

'Then he was a bit of a scapegoat. And there was a particular interview on SBS with Craig Foster. It was a brutal, brutal moment for Ange. Then he was spat out basically. And he wasn't doing much; he went to Greece. Now, we know how that ended, you know, a lower league club, he's walked away, he's come back to Australia unemployed. No one wanted to touch him. He was coaching kids in parks. It was a very tough time.

'I remember catching up with him at the time. He's not wanting to show his full colours. No one ever knows what Ange is thinking. I don't know if you've caught that sense. He'll never tell you what he is thinking, truly. He's probably got two or three friends that are close to him. As much as he was struggling at the time, he wouldn't tell you. You know what I mean?

'And he ended up finally getting a role in the A-League with Brisbane Roar. And that was, again, sheer luck because the league manager at the time, Ange went up to him one day at a game and said: 'I'm looking to coach again, if you see an opportunity in the A-League, let me know.' And a couple of weeks later, the coach at the time of Brisbane Roar, Frank Farina, got caught drunk-driving and they had to let go of him. And the manager of the A-League suggests to Brisbane Roar: 'I think I've got a manager for you; give Ange the opportunity.' The rest is history? Not only was it history, but he went there, and he created a club that played the most exciting football you'll ever see. They won three championships in a row, because he created a particular style: fast, furious, entertaining. And that was typical of Ange. Then the rest is history because he obviously goes to Melbourne Victory, then the Socceroos job – his second tenure with our federation and probably, again, he didn't get the support he needed from the federation.'

That's a story for another chapter. Another example of the demands Postecoglou puts not only on those who work for him, but on the line managers, executive officers and board members who are technically his superiors. The only thing tougher than being one of his players might be working as his nominal 'boss' in any organisation. That part of him hasn't changed. Even if, in some ways, he has mellowed.

For the record, Postecoglou and Foster have since been reconciled, with the pair even able to joke about their famous fall-out. A little bit, anyway. Dig a little deeper and you'll find that neither is willing to give ground on the actual bones of the matter, with 'Fozzy' insisting that he was right to ask the tough questions and Ange equally certain that the interview went too far. Both can afford to be magnanimous about it now, given how things have worked out, with Foster now earning widespread plaudits not merely for his punditry but his work with refugees. And Postecoglou a long way from the dark, cold and lonely wilderness into which he was cast back in 2007.

Key Game

BRISBANE ROAR 2 PERTH GLORY 1

Suncorp Stadium, Brisbane
22 April 2012

THERE has been so much focus on Ange Postecoglou's stylistic achievements at Brisbane that people occasionally overlook the substance of what he did, with victory in the 2012 Grand Final making Roar the first A-League team ever to win back-to-back titles. The fact that they did it while playing in a manner dubbed 'Roarcelona' by supporters made it all the sweeter.

According to those who were a part of this success, however, the aftermath of this second straight final win provided an insight into what we might call the Alex Ferguson side of Postecoglou's personality. Older readers will vividly recall Fergie laying into his Aberdeen players, live on television, after they'd just beaten Rangers to win the Scottish Cup at Hampden in 1983. Those not old enough to have witnessed it live can find it easily enough on YouTube. It's astonishing. Borderline unhinged. But it's been generally regarded as a sign of the ridiculously unbending nature, the insistence upon raising standards ever higher, that made Fergie such a managerial legend.

By the time Brisbane arrived at their second straight Grand Final, Postecoglou had already overcome early doubts – another recurring theme – to achieve unprecedented greatness, leading the Roar to an Australian record

– across any club sport – of 36 games without defeat between September 2010 and November 2011.

Interestingly, however, they'd finished runners-up in the league in that second season. Champions by dint of their triumph in a play-off system introduced in the mid-1980s, no one doubted their claim upon the title; this is just how Aussie sport works, with the Grand Final winners deemed undisputed champions. While the Brisbane players were still celebrating, however, Postecoglou took an opportunity to put a slightly different spin on the occasion.

Thomas Broich, a key figure for Roar, revealed: 'Before he sent us off on our break, he spoke to the players. And this was just after we won the championship, remember. He looked us in the eye and said: "If you think it's good enough to come second in this league, think again." So it was like: "Congrats on winning the championship but . . ." He was so upset about us not winning the league to go with the title, like that was a failure to him. That's his standard. He's relentless. And only perfection will do. He can be very, very grumpy, actually. It's not easy to satisfy him. You really have to play the best football, the hardest way you can – and then he might walk off the pitch with a smile. Might!'

Chapter 7

AHEAD OF THE CURVE

ANGE Postecoglou isn't taking some wild punt based on blind faith. He's meticulously planning a revolution. Identifying weak points in less resilient, more inflexible game models. And plotting a strategy for total victory. Armed with the sort of advanced intelligence that, if history is any judge, usually gives him a jump start on the crowd. Ahead of the curve? There have been times, according to many who have worked with Postecoglou, when it felt as if he was plotting an entirely new parabola – one drawing on old sightlines and guide marks, admittedly – in indelible ink.

'It's about being the better team, rather than just beating the better team,' is how one of his most qualified former players, Thomas Broich, rather brilliantly explains the philosophy. Now something of a tactical guru in his own right, the German knows that any coach can get lucky by 'masterminding' a cup upset or fluke win against all odds. But that's not the Postecoglou way. His old gaffer, Broich insists, believes there is a more complete, more deserving, more likely sort of triumph to be had, even against the very best teams on the planet, for those smart enough and brave enough to commit to the cause.

So do not ever make the mistake of dismissing his tendency to double down as the mark of an inveterate gambler, pathologically unable to tear himself away from the gaming tables as he succumbs to the desperate desire for another dopamine hit. In his eyes, he's always betting on a sure thing. If everyone needs a bit of luck to succeed in a chaotic game like football, Postecoglou's tactics – a twist on the flexible 4-3-3 model adopted and adapted by everyone from Rinus Michels to Johan Cruyff, Marcello Lippi to Pep Guardiola's golden-era Barca – represent a statement of practical intent, as well as an expression of aesthetic ambition. He's not hiding behind principles in the hope that no one notices the odd blow-out defeat hidden behind all those pretty patterns. He knows, with a certainty far surpassing opinion or even belief, that this approach to football gives him the greatest chance of achieving consistent success.

And should you wish to argue about his methods? Well, as the kids these days might put it, he's kept the receipts. The most convincing relate to the utterly ludicrous transformation job he performed at Brisbane Roar, for whom he delivered back-to-back titles, a pretty nifty nickname – Roarcelona after, well, y'know – and a place in Australian sporting folklore, courtesy of a 36-game undefeated streak that stands, to this day, as a record.

Like any good agent of change, what he did in Brisbane scared people. Inspired more than a few, as well. But definitely caused a few tremors of uncertainty and apprehension. That was certainly the vibe in the Roar dressing room, with even some of his most ardent admirers still trembling at the memory of being highlighted during brutally clinical video analysis sessions. The recollection of being singled out for cold-eyed criticism can still trigger a flashback or two among those put on the spot. Yet these very same men also talk, with enormous pride, about the feeling of invincibility generated by Postecoglou, a man intent on educating his players on the finer details of tactical nuances in the final third – and predicting the advance of expected goal metrics by making them understand that not all scoring chances are created equal. They marvel at how he made true believers out of most. And cleared out almost an entire starting XI of footballers who either couldn't or wouldn't take the pledge of allegiance to quick rotations, lateral movement and burying opponents under an avalanche of passing combinations.

Dropped into a messy situation after spending almost two years away from the elite end of Aussie soccer, Postecoglou – appointed to the Brisbane job in October 2009 as a replacement for former Socceroos boss Frank Farina, who had been sacked in the wake of a drink-driving offence – certainly didn't take a half-assed approach to his shot at redemption, overhauling the squad and imposing an entirely new style in a league still dominated by old British traditions. Out went all thoughts of hoofing the ball into the final third, making the other lot play facing their own goal, and fighting for the right to play anything approaching beautiful football. Many of the players he binned, among them well-known names (to a Scottish audience) such as Charlie Miller, Craig Moore and Bob Malcolm, were mainstays and fan favourites. The kind of battle-hardened characters, mainstream logic held, who would be needed by a manager most famous, at this point, for his televised tiff with Craig Foster two and a half years earlier.

Couldn't they all just get along? Or at least come to some sort of professional agreement? After all, personality clashes have been a part of sport since one village challenged the neighbouring hamlet to a game of this foteball [*sic*] lark; you can guarantee that the first captain of Little Cockup disagreed with his gaffer's unnecessarily strict policy on the use of cudgels – defenders only, no deliberate aiming for the tender parts – for the derby against Great Bottom-on-the-Rump. As the great American baseball coach Casey Stengel once put it, management is about keeping the players who hate you away from the guys who haven't made up their mind yet.

But this wasn't about simply learning to work with others. It was a battle of wills over how the game should be played. How it had to be played. Postecoglou began by convincing players that it would actually be easier to play a more intricate passing game, if only they were to give it a try, because even the least talented among them could play a five-yard pass. Like all good managers, he didn't ask players to perform feats beyond their ability – but did force them to reconsider their limits, technically and tactically, physically and mentally. The results, in time, were astonishing.

Former Germany Under-21 star and A-League legend Broich, whose post-playing career saw him become a respected analyst for Bundesliga TV before moving on to the technical staff at Union Berlin, has spent years breaking down tactics and formations, movements and counter-movements, in a bid to fulfil the ultimate goal of any good professional observer – identifying the rare signs of order and intelligent design amid the mayhem of a game with 22 players and about 18 million variables. Signed by Postecoglou for the Roar, Broich finds it hard to describe just how radical his old gaffer's plans were. So he starts with the nuts and bolts. And a neat summation of the safety-first thinking that his old boss consigned to the bin in Brisbane.

'Sure, against the very best, you can hit them on the break and on a lucky day, you get the result,' he said, adding: 'Ange is not interested in that. He wants to take his team to a point where he can go anyplace basically and say: "Well, we want to boss the game, create our own luck and we want to be able to beat that team by being better than them." He does that away to Real Madrid. If that isn't inspiring . . . He inspires me every day, even now, in my daily work.

'What I can tell you about, wherever he's been, are the cornerstones of his game. And, with us, it was about numerical superiority around the ball. So, in possession we had a lot of guys showing for the ball because, clearly, his idea is that football was based on basically saying it's super complicated to play a 50-yard diagonal ball. But even quite average footballers should be able to pass the ball seven, eight metres to support each other, protect the ball, give options, provide angles and little triangles. The whole football model was based on that and the rotations that happened, they were to shift the opposition – for us, the No.6 dropping deep to make it a back three, like a 3-6-1 system. The wingers would tuck inside as a right-footed winger playing on the left and almost play like a No.10 who would arrive quite late; the No.8 then peels to the side. Those rotations constantly put the opposition in doubt and gave us great numbers.'

Getting bodies in position is one thing. Preparing them to make the right choices quite another. Nowadays, any elite coach worth his salt can simply message his in-house data analyst with a request for hard numbers to reinforce the message. Pair that with some appropriate match footage and the modern player will have no excuse for failing to understand. In 2009, few in football had even heard of xG (expected goals), never mind xA (expected assists), PPDA (passes per defensive action) or any of the other myriad abbreviations that are now common industry language.

Broich said: 'There was another really important thing, the last one, when we were around the final third. Basically, he was really ahead of his time, in terms of expected goals and all that. It wasn't a thing back then, but we clearly had entry points, and he knew very specifically where he wanted the ball played through – always between the full back and the centre half – and that's basically the penetrating pass into the danger zone. The idea was to then just put it in and it's basically a tap-in goal. Also, when it came to crossing or shooting from distance? Not an option. It was important to recycle the ball and go to the other side to try your luck there, to find an entry point, and if it didn't happen, we had to shift again, and again, and again.

'If you think about it, he just understood the numbers. It's not the best option to knock a ball in from the touchline and hope for the best with a header or to shoot from distance – we all know the xG value of that. It was about getting behind their backline then creating a better opportunity.'

At Celtic, of course, Postecoglou merely demonstrated the latest incarnation of his ever-evolving game model. He doesn't tinker much with his formation. But that doesn't mean his team can't change things up. Who he picks to play in specific positions in the 4-3-3 makes all the difference to the manager, who knows full well that Daizen Maeda and Jota take wildly varying approaches to playing on the left wing, and that Reo Hatate is not the same sort of No.8 as Matt O'Riley. Aaron Mooy is a different type in his own right.

Think of how often we saw his Celtic team convert a low cross from close range, however, and you'll recognise echoes of the xG-predicting model implemented at Brisbane, before being carried to Melbourne Victory, Australia and then Yokohama F. Marinos. Under Ange, the Scottish champions lived for those 'entry point' balls that set up a simple cross-and-finish exercise for whoever happens to be bursting into the box at the right moment.

With the ball, Postecoglou was one of the first to adopt the full five-lane approach to attacking. Which is exactly what it sounds like; imagine the opposition final third divided into five lanes lengthways, then make sure that you have a player in every single lane. Because he pushes his full backs up and infield alongside his No.6, just for starters, Celtic effectively went at teams with a 2-3-5 formation, with both of their more advanced midfielders able to join the front three in a full-width shape that gives defending teams all kinds of conniptions. In an era of compact defences and shutting off inside lanes, you can't possibly cover a team spread out with such width. Something has to give.

Which is why Celtic, no slouches on the counter-attack when opportunity presents itself, could show such patience against domestic opponents, in particular. If the opposition stayed narrow, Postecoglou's men would generate a one-on-one for either winger. Given the gulf in ability between the likes of Jota, Maeda, Liel Abada etc. and 90 per cent of full backs in the Scottish Premiership, coaches like to call that a technical advantage. Pretty self-explanatory. If that wasn't an option, they'd overload one side of the box – often after a quick switch of play that left defenders struggling to shuffle across – and generate a more obvious numerical advantage. Should none of the above work, well, there was always the movement. So much movement. A No.8 darting in and out of the box, dragging his marker with him, only for one of the full backs to leave his advanced central midfield position and make an underlapping run. Whatever the exact details of the combination, however many rotations Postecoglou may have thrown into the mix, the final phase of play often involved a seemingly simple diagonal run, a straight pass, a driven low cross and a finish by someone like main striker Kyogo Furuhashi, whose movement and wit provided another essential element of Ange-ball, namely a centre forward who understood the work required to generate space for others.

Counter-pressing was another element of Celtic's approach that gained a lot of attention in the domestic game.

The 'rest defence' – the term used to describe an attacking team's structure upon losing the ball that enables a swift and positive transition into counter-pressing – was built upon Callum McGregor and one of the advanced full backs. The covering presence of central defender Cameron

Carter-Vickers as a sort of human cheat code, in Scottish Premiership terms, was another vital component – meaning they could risk squeezing up on opponents if/when the ball was lost in the attacking third of the pitch.

As much as they liked to get after opposing defences, particularly in a domestic setting, they could drop back into a 4-5-1 when necessary. That's been one of the trends in the Champions League in recent seasons, for clubs with much greater resources than Celtic, with high-intensity pressing giving way to medium blocks in many instances.

Everything Postecoglou does is about overloading the opposition, with the ultimate aim being to present some hapless defender with a choice between a bad and a catastrophic option. It requires a lot of moving parts. And even one player misfiring can have serious consequences. Mastering his style, then, requires a lot of dedication, as players learn their own roles and that of their team-mates.

Summing up his philosophy in a webinar for coaches organised by analysis firm Hudl in 2020, Postecoglou offered up a fascinating insight into the key performance indicators – passes completed and possession stats but also how quickly his team regain possession, and where they do it – that help him go much deeper into the why, as well as the what, of any game. Every time he's made a tweak or a change, it has been to enhance, never dilute, his core principles. And it's all designed to keep him one step ahead of the opposition.

'I've always tried to coach in the future,' he revealed, adding: 'I'm building teams for five years' time. If I follow the current trend, I'll be copying everyone else. I want to do something no one else is doing.

Above. A new era. Ange Postecoglou grew up on a diet of English football and its most famous clubs. The opportunity to join Tottenham Hotspur in the summer of 2023 provided the chance to test himself in exalted company and to put his own distinctive stamp on a club in need of a coaching revolution.
Tottenham Hotspur FC via Getty Images

Left. All action. A distinguished playing career in the Australian domestic game brought international honours at youth level – and four full Socceroos caps – for the energetic star, pictured in action for South Melbourne in 1990.
Craig Borrow/Newspix

Master and apprentice. Postecoglou and Steve Blair (right) join Real Madrid legend Ferenc Puskás – the South Melbourne coach who would play such a huge part in his young captain's understanding of the game – in celebrating their 1991 Grand Final victory.

Limping along. Postecoglou's career was cut short by injury. He's pictured here, on crutches, with team-mate Steve Blair and then South Melbourne president George Vasilopoulos.

Above. Down time. Coach Postecoglou, current South Melbourne president Nicholas Maikousis (then just a young director, left) and long-standing director/former vice president Bill Georgantis (centre) relax in Fiji ahead of the Australian champions winning the 1999 Oceania Club Championship.

Left. Roarcelona. Grand Final success with Brisbane Roar was delivered in style as the rising coach brought his swashbuckling approach to the fore. Postecoglou and his Roar skipper Matthew Smith are pictured during the ticker-tape parade through the centre of the city as fans greeted their heroes.

Dan Peled / Alamy Stock Photo

Golden days. Success in the 2015 Asian Cup final was a significant achievement for the budding international manager, pictured here with star player Tim Cahill after guiding his side to victory in that defining match against South Korea. Nippon News / Alamy Stock Photo

City slickers. Postecoglou became part of a global coaching dynasty when he joined Yokohama F Marinos in Japan, part of the City Football Group. He is pictured here with Manchester City counterpart Pep Guardiola, Blues player Phil Foden and Yokohama midfielder Takuya Kida prior to a friendly between the two sides in 2019.

B.J. Warnick / Alamy Stock Photo

Paradise found. The summer of 2021 brought the unveiling of Celtic's new manager as the Glasgow giants sought to regroup and rebuild after a period of turmoil. The new man at the helm brought fresh ideas and a steely determination to succeed in one of football's most unforgiving cities. Jeff Holmes / Alamy Stock Photo

A Celtic initiation. Postecoglou and pal Steve Blair – who continually pushed the merits of Celtic to his Liverpool-supporting South Melbourne team-mate during their playing days – pose at the main entrance to Celtic Park during a visit in the summer of 1993.
Courtesy of Steve Blair

Room for a little one? Looking like a young Billy Connolly, the grinning tourist mugs for a shot at one of the old-fashioned Celtic Park turnstiles during his trip as an aspiring Aussie coach on holiday in Scotland. Three decades or so later, he'd be walking through the front door as manager. Courtesy of Steve Blair

If the shirt fits. Postecoglou poses in front of a memorabilia display during his tour of Celtic Park in 1993. Courtesy of Steve Blair

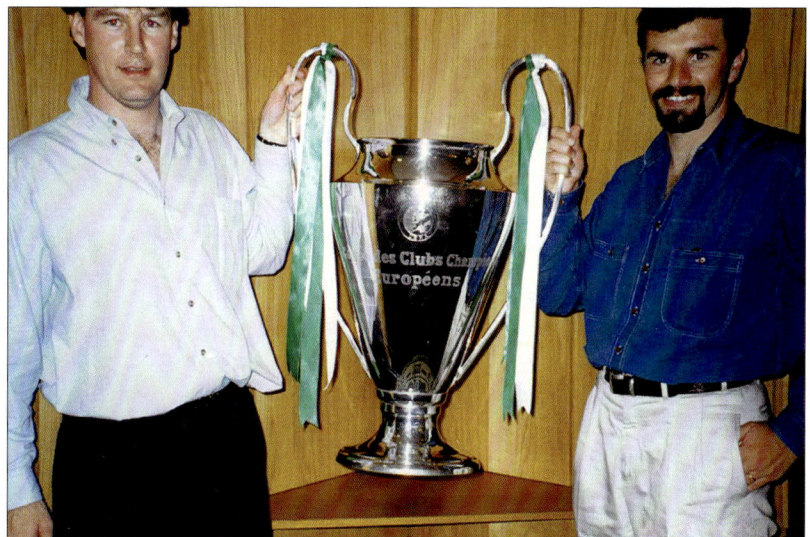

Living the dream. A young Ange and close pal Steve Blair hold aloft the replica European Cup – a memento of Celtic becoming the first British club to lift the 'cup with the big ears' in 1967 – during their visit to Celtic Park. Little did anyone know that he would one day lead the Hoops into the Champions League. Courtesy of Steve Blair

Make mine a treble. Postecoglou raises the Scottish Cup at Hampden Park after victory over Inverness Caledonian Thistle in what proved to be his final match as Celtic manager. The move to Tottenham was announced just days later, on the back of a domestic clean sweep with the Hoops. Sportimage / Alamy Stock Photo

New names, same approach. The move to the English Premier League provided the opportunity to work with an all-star cast. For Postecoglou the principles that earned him his shot with Spurs never faltered through the highs and lows of his debut season with the club. Kieran Cleeves / Sportimage Ltd / Alamy Live News

We're loving big Ange instead. The Postecoglou style quickly won admirers in north London, the Spurs fans expressing their love of their new boss in song with a football adaptation of the 1990s Robbie Williams hit 'Angels'. David Klein / Sportimage Ltd / Alamy Live News

'The game is constantly evolving. People tend to follow those trends. I'd rather go beyond that. What's the next phase? People looked at Pep's Barcelona and came up with a counter-pressing, uptempo game. That's the beauty of the game.

'But my utopia is still going back to the 1974 World Cup and Total Football, freeing players of positional constrictions. The more we can do that, the happier I get – but the crazier it gets. Can we get to a stage where players don't think of themselves as defenders or midfielders or attackers? Can we get our game even more fluid, because players don't say: "I'm a centre back; I have to be in this area."

'That's the way the game will eventually head to at some certain point. When it gets to that point of my utopia, someone will come up with a real rigid system to stop it and we'll go back again.'

At Brisbane, the most willing converts threw themselves headlong into the Ange-ball project with almost religious dedication. Those who railed against the new thinking, naturally, didn't last long. Unfortunately for Postecoglou, some of the departed then started pissing back into the tent via a media not exactly overstuffed with friends of Ange; he faced a barrage of scepticism and criticism before he'd even settled into his role. Sound familiar? Then, as now, he refused to let the outside noise divert him so much as half a degree from his set course.

Broich credits Postecoglou's ability to tell a story, a rousing tale placing players in the role of heroes, as crucial to what he achieves as a man manager. Even more important, naturally, is producing some early proofs to strengthen the credibility of his theories.

'The most important thing is to demonstrate that it works, which will not happen straight away – but that's when you really get people to buy it,' said Broich. 'It's really important to point out early successes. You may not be there quite yet, but to be able to show progress is super important. He's a master of video analysis, which is a key component, I guess. Another one is storytelling, the whole "dare to be different" thing. Like, imagine if we went on the road less travelled, where we could end up. You know, just inspiring people. But then at the right time be very "my way or the highway"; it's a combination of these two things, which are quite contrary if you think about it. To inspire them, to give them the opportunity to just be a follower, to just buy in. But the people who were too sceptical or maybe were working against the whole thing – you know, at a football club there's a lot of people who say "this can't work" or "this is too risky, this is ridiculous" – there comes a point when you have to say: "Well, either you're in or you're out." And he's got a great combination of these things.

'We had a few signings from abroad who didn't like the style, the intensity or the demands. Even though he'd brought some of them in and they were foreign players, which means they usually cost more money than the Aussie boys, if he gets the feeling there's too much resistance from guys, if they're not willing to change, he'll get rid of them.'

Despite his own status as a confirmed disciple of Postecoglou, Broich retains some sympathy for those who simply couldn't cut it, saying: 'It's a normal phenomenon in older players; you're used to playing a certain style and, at the age of 32, there comes a guy that tells you no more long balls from now on. Now you've got a centre half who's got to play like Gerard Piqué at the time. A lot of guys, they oppose that kind of approach, bringing a bad vibe to the dressing room and he just had to get rid of them.

'Something I admire about him, because of his approach, he is under criticism a lot of the time. Not now, of course, when it works, but early on at Celtic – and at Brisbane. It's so admirable how he handles pressure. You probably know his story with the Young Socceroos when he was humiliated on live television. And I think that day was a game changer for him. From then on, he was going to do things differently. But, when he started doing it, he had to overcome so much resistance.

'In the beginning, there weren't many believers, and he was constantly going to the next, bigger level. Even after what he did with Brisbane. Everyone was always saying, "That was Brisbane, now it's Melbourne Victory . . ." Or they would say: "That was club football, now it's the national team." Then it became "this is the Japanese league" and then "there's no way you can do that in Europe . . ." People constantly doubting him. So for him to find that energy or, more so, that conviction to believe in himself and being able to handle all the bad press and criticism . . .

'A lot of the guys he got rid of went on to become journalists in Brisbane; they turned into media experts and pundits. For weeks and months, they'd hammer him in public and there was nothing he could do about it because the results weren't quite there. And every weekend, he'd have to read you're not good enough as a coach, a good enough man manager, or good enough with tactics. It didn't break him – quite the contrary. He just got stronger, and you need someone that strong to be a real leader.

'He basically said if Plan A doesn't work, make it better. Even to this day, I hear so many people talking about Plan B and C and D, and what if the opposition play that kind of football or pressure like that? Playing styles constantly change, but not with him. Regardless of results – even in the beginning when we didn't have success or went through a rough patch when we lost a few games – he would not change his style; there was never any room for doubt and to me, that's key. Because other coaches have similar ideas and want to play out from the back, but there comes a point really when they say: "Yeah, we conceded two goals in the last five games trying to play out from the back and if you realise the pressure is just a little too much, you're allowed to play a long ball . . ." or even frame it differently, like: "It's super important to turn them around and play a few balls over the top and it'll help us later in the game." No, it doesn't! All it does is, you get a free pass basically to play long balls, and players *love* that: "Oh, I'm under pressure, I'll play a long ball." '

Broich laughs as he describes the very human tendency of players to take the easy option, should the manager give them permission in advance. Never provide players with an excuse for failure, right? Don't even throw in the suggestion of a cop-out, no matter how extreme the circumstances. Postecoglou understands this. And, although many of his former players mention the fact that no two team talks were ever the same, he always had favourite themes. He isn't afraid to harp on about key points. Especially when armed with video evidence to press home his argument.

Asked what it was like to have your name called out during those analysis sessions, former No.10 Broich let out a roar of laughter as he admitted: 'I'd tense up right away. It was never personal; it was never to have a go at anyone. For me, for instance, did I move at the right time? Did I get the turn in? It was about being brave because, as a player, you always think you're under a lot of pressure. Even though someone is ten metres from you, as soon as he's looking towards you it's like: "He's going to take the ball off me so I'm going to play it safe and shift the ball." It was all about getting turns in because for his football, he needed those little pockets and vertical passes. Like an accelerator, because we'd move the ball patiently and eventually when there's an opening you can't waste those opportunities.

'It took me a while to really master that, and it was actually really helpful to go through those analysis sessions because I realised I had a very different perception compared to the actual game. He was really good at highlighting and pointing out: "Look at this, there's plenty of space. I expect you to turn there," or "show earlier to get a rotation going." It was like that, and it wasn't always pleasant to go through this because I was too scared to go for that turn again, and again, and again.

'To be honest with you, we were shit scared of video analysis, but at the same time it was a learning tool. He would never, ever take you out of the team for making a mistake if you followed the plan. He would show you the way you went wrong, and what he expected of you, and where you need to be better, but then he'd play you again. And, to me, for the first time in my football career, this became a learning opportunity.

'It was a way for him to communicate his idea to everyone because, even though we weren't addressed in a specific clip, it'd apply to you as well and it'd fit into the bigger picture. Especially when it came to being brave and playing out from the back; I was an attacker, so I didn't think that affected me as much. So, if he hammered a centre half, I was like: "So what? I'm just glad it wasn't me!" But I did realise how it all comes together; it's a puzzle in the end because the centre half needs us up front to provide options and he needs us to be supportive of what he's doing.

'That was another really key ingredient, especially when the guys at the back – goalkeepers, centre halves, No.6s – they had to play through a lot of pressure and it was unfamiliar territory for them, and he backed them to an extent that was unbelievable at times. He would accept their mistakes if they were just brave and doing the right thing. To us, it was also a very strong message.'

Postecoglou himself is nothing if not consistent in his messaging, both in public and in private, with plenty of chat about sticking to core principles. He credited his Celtic players, just as he heaped praise upon the guys who put in the hard yards at his other previous clubs, with creating an environment that imposes demands on everyone. Including the coaching staff. Even in their most comfortable victories, he pointed out, you'd see Celtic being aggressive until the sound of the final whistle. That's not by chance. Players working under his regime are quickly conditioned to think in such terms. And, when things get tight and the opposition are countering every punch from each new angle, they never seem to sink into the 'just one of those days' mindset that turns many a would-be champion into an also-ran.

On a personal level, Postecoglou points out that he tries to stay even-tempered regardless of goals scored or conceded, even revealing – in December 2022 – some quite extreme methodology to maintain focus on the important things, saying: 'When we do our analysis, we do it in the absence of the scoreboard and what it shows up there. We just look purely at the football we play and the kind of team we want to be.'

Now, if some managers came out with that sort of line, the response from the Scottish public, in particular, would have been a pithy and succinct: 'Aye, right.' With Postecoglou, though, it's entirely believable. Because it's balanced by a relentless pursuit of points and trophies, as he explained: 'It's no different from anywhere else. I'm not happy if we're not winning. From our perspective, there's a clear understanding – we need to get results. We need to win games of football. But I want to win games playing a certain way and playing our style. I don't want to win games by accident or with a stroke of luck. I don't think that fills us with belief.'

And so he carries on. Working on a style of play where, to sum up one of his key points, he could probably start his left or right back in central midfield without a player or a member of the coaching staff batting an eyelid. Nothing he's achieved, certainly since the Brisbane days, has been by chance. The fact that he's made a variation on this model work with the Roar, Victory, the Socceroos, Yokohama and Celtic is testament enough to its durability, surely, to win over the most sceptical of naysayers.

Old friend Peter Filopoulos, who has been in and around Australian football his entire adult life, tells a story that sums up both the reluctance of some to believe what they were seeing, and the ability of Postecoglou to confound the harshest critics, the Football Australia head of marketing, communications and corporate affairs saying: 'When he got up to Brisbane, we gave Brisbane a name. Every Grand Final we got an opportunity, we'd be there. We created the banner: "Thank you Ange for Roarcelona." We made the name Roarcelona because he brought in the Barcelona flavour at the time. And so, we gave it a name.

'Whenever we went to a pub, a local pub here in Melbourne, and their game was on, the Brisbane game, we would share our thoughts with people about it. We were really advertising him as much as we could down here in Melbourne! And then I remember Brisbane were playing Melbourne Victory and some of my closest friends – in the hierarchy at Melbourne Victory at the time – being shocked because I've turned up to the game, you know, in an orange Brisbane Roar top. Jeez, they weren't happy. But as it turns out, you know, two years later they said: "I think you're right, we're gonna get him as a coach here." So, they actually signed them up as a coach for Melbourne Victory. Ange has always been ahead of his time. Then we saw it play out at Celtic.'

Chapter 8

I KNOW WHAT I LIKE

GIVEN the human brain's love of patterns, real or imagined, it's easy enough to identify recurring similarities and repeating sequences among the hundreds of recruitment decisions made by Ange Postecoglou over the course of a long managerial career. Like any attempt to apply logic in a game like football, however, studying hours of video footage, mountains of stats and hours of testimony from those involved will most likely stretch the sanity of the searcher to breaking point. Without providing specific evidence of some hitherto-undiscovered X factor shared by all who merit the Postecoglou seal of approval.

The closest you might get, by spending time looking, listening and learning from those who have worked with this elite coach over the years, is an understanding that there's some sort of character trait he seeks in players. Not just a winning mentality; we could paper a path from Melbourne to London, via Glasgow and Yokohama, with the words of managers and coaches expounding upon the need to sign 'winners' who have developed the emotional resilience that might help Team A clinch the title/avoid relegation/keep the board happy for another six months. But adaptability, maybe? An aptitude for learning? A willingness to stay the course when your supporters, your mates, maybe even your agent, is wondering what on earth the gaffer is playing at? Something like that. Almost. Kind of.

The truth is that Postecoglou is, of course, very precise about what he wants from every signing, with his adherence to a mandated playing style acting as an automatic filter in a market flooded with footballers who can, on average, do seven or eight out of ten things brilliantly. If the two or three elements beyond them mean they'll struggle with the speed of thought and movement required to play for the man, they're simply not considered.

Among those who believe the answer to life, the universe and everything can be found simply by mining deeply enough into the data, meanwhile, there's an enduring fascination with those players released, sold or sent on a hook-slinging exercise by a coach with high standards and specific demands. The guys who either wouldn't or couldn't fall into line with Ange-ball, a philosophy that extends far beyond the 90-odd minutes of actual match action? Our need to create order amid the chaos means we can always find some shared trait – a fault, a flaw, even just a stylistic quirk – that unites them.

On the occasions when he's spoken in any depth about recruitment, the man himself has discussed knowing exactly what he wants in a certain player to fill each position on the pitch. And what he's looking for in terms of squad depth. He knows what he likes, in other words.

Postecoglou also mentions his gut quite frequently, especially when it comes to deciding if a footballer has the less tangible qualities needed to succeed in a specific environment. Maybe he's got some super-intelligent 'good bacteria' guiding him towards the right decision?

Nick Deligiannis is something of an expert in finding talented individuals to fill particular roles, with his role on the board of a major recruitment company testament to his insight and experience in weeding out the flashy from the substantial, the seemingly competent from the truly valuable potential employees. The former Heidelberg United forward is also another of Postecoglou's inner circle, a lifelong friend who sees obvious similarities between the corporate world of hiring and firing, and the necessity to make good decisions when building a football team.

Explaining what he's learned from Ange, he said: 'Ability and attitude are super important and there can be no compromise on that, of course. That's just standard in football. They have to be able to play at a certain standard, in a certain way.

'But he will never try to squeeze someone who doesn't fit in culturally. Never, ever. That's everything in recruitment for Ange. Because the culture and environment are everything. That's why he did so well – again – at Celtic. Everyone, even if they're not playing, you can see that they've bought into the team culture, the club culture, the idea that it's bigger than any one of us. He's so big on that. If anyone doesn't fit that . . .

'He's given me examples of players who didn't fit the bill – and they don't last. Again, he's not disrespectful. But if they don't fit the culture he wants to instil in the team, if they're not right for the environment, that won't work. So that's what he looks for, as well as the technical ability. It's so important to him.'

That ability to fit in is obviously a factor in any healthy workplace environment, even if football has a long – and proud? – history of tolerating oddballs, crackpots, alcoholics, gambling addicts, violent criminals, artistic geniuses who see the world from a different angle ... the entire range, from the lunatic fringe to the most extreme end of the creative spectrum, can be found somewhere within the beautiful game. When Postecoglou talks about a certain type, then, you have to remember that the sport's parameters – its leeway when it comes to fitting some identikit model of a modern footballer – are a little looser than the average HR department might usually allow.

Yet it is a fact that Ange has emptied job lots of players deemed unsuitable to the job, with his arrival at Brisbane Roar precipitating the departure of some big names and marquee signings, a pattern that has been repeated ever since. And he's shown himself to be astute in replacing the departed misfits with guys who slot right into place. Using every advantage at his disposal to gain an edge in the market.

'He's just taking the piss, with his recruitment from the J.League,' is how Colin Chambers, educational director at the International Professional Scouting Organisation describes Postecoglou's operations in the Japanese market, in particular, the experienced talent spotter adding: 'That's a perfect example of a manager knowing the market – and knowing what he's looking for. He's just dangling his fishing rod into the pool, aiming for specific targets, knowing that they'll bite because they know him, either because they've played under him at Yokohama, or they know someone who did. It's a bit of market mastery, to be honest.'

A lot of interest in the Aussie's methods obviously focuses on his recruitment from Japan and, in another market he flagged up as being of interest even before he'd got his first transfer window at Celtic completed, South Korea. He has always resisted attempts to lump his signings from this part of the world together in some sort of job lot, stressing their individual strengths and weaknesses, characters and personalities. It would be stupid, bordering on offensive, to suggest that all Japanese or Korean players play in a specific manner. As silly as suggesting that Portuguese winger Jota was cut from the same stock as Canadian full back Alistair Johnston.

In theory, virtually any middle-market European club of middling to modest means could have gone to Vissel Kobe with a bid that would have landed Kyogo Furuhashi, a 26-year-old striker who had played all his club football in Japan. In this age of remote scouting, everyone has access to the same footage, the same statistics, the same mountain of information that is supposed to enhance talent identification. If used correctly.

All too often, however, modern scouting departments are so overwhelmed with data and input that they risk paralysis by analysis. Ultimately, someone has to greenlight a move for some of the targets on the board. Yet everyone in the process is wary of succumbing to what the NASA control room boys called 'Go Fever' – allowing the emotion of launch to override what the numbers were telling them, because they don't want to be the guy to abort the mission.

Speak to any veteran manager and they'll tell you any number of horror stories about the time they backed the judgement of some respected scout or trusted assistant, only to be landed with a player entirely unsuitable for the job. It's a personal decision, in the end. No matter how many sporting directors or heads of recruitment might be pushing a potential recruit, the gaffer has to feel good about any new arrival.

What helps Postecoglou, in particular, when it comes to dealing with his recruitment staff? Once again, we go back to lessons learned in his first managerial job at South Melbourne. Where the scouting operation, in general, amounted to the gaffer keeping an eye on league rivals, assessing players not just for their ability but their suitability, then asking someone on the board to make a move.

Peter Filopoulos, his old general manager at South, explained: 'He always had a pretty strong sense of the team he wanted. He was always able to identify what he didn't have. And he wouldn't tell you too much. He would never tell you too much.

'So, he'd say to me: "Big fella. I want you to come with me this weekend. I'm gonna go see a couple of games." He just wants to hang out with me, right? We'd go watch a game. He wouldn't tell me what he's thinking during the game, and then on the way home he'd go: "I want you to bring us that player, number 2, Stevie Iosifidis. I think I want to recruit him." So I just did the deal – but he wouldn't tell me beforehand. And he always made the signing because that person filled a role.'

If we consider Brisbane Roar as the beginning of Ange's 'second act' as a manager, it's worth looking at the sheer scale of incomings and outgoings of players during that period of rebirth and rediscovered success. And it's important to note how badly the quick-fire revolution went down with supporters and pundits; there was plenty of pearl clutching about the new gaffer cutting loose top talents like Tommy Oar, Adam Sarota and Michael Zullo, while also clearing the decks of veterans Craig Moore, Charlie Miller, Liam Reddy, Bob Malcolm and Danny Tiatto. The stance taken with popular veteran Moore, in particular, put Postecoglou in direct conflict with much of the squad. In the end, he issued an ultimatum to the board – who backed the new manager and allowed former Socceroos star Moore to move on, ironically enough, to Greek club Kavala.

Former Rangers player Miller, who was the A-League's reigning overseas player of the year and still just 33 when he left Brisbane, has since admitted that he – like many others – misjudged a coach who was still thought of, by the majority, as that former Young Socceroos gaffer who blew his top on TV. Because Postecoglou was openly mocked in sections of the media for some of the signings made after he took over from Frank Farina. It didn't help that Farina had a weekly column in *The Courier-Mail*. Which he used, not infrequently, to question what the hell Ange was doing to 'his' squad, chucking out all the good guys and leaders, their places taken by no-names and, increasingly, youngsters who might not have been granted game time under a less bold boss.

The fact that Postecoglou had worked with the Young Socceroos, seeing up close the raw talent given fewer and fewer opportunities for refinement in a domestic league dominated by hardened battlers and foreign veterans, is identified by many as a key factor in developing his eye for a player. And the wit required to imagine how any new recruit might fit into his plans.

'The big advantage I've noticed over time, and this applies to Ange as much as it does to someone like Pep Guardiola, is the history of working with younger players,' is how Nick Dimitrakis, who saw Postecoglou work with kids as young as 11 at Nunawading FC, puts it. 'Their philosophy has translated from youth into seniors. And it's easier for them to identify the right player coming in at youth level into senior level to fill the role, to complement the philosophy here or the position. So, that's a big advantage.

'I've known coaches that have been good, but don't have that ability to know which young players to promote. So, identification is a big thing. You see a lot of good players going missing out of the game. I think identification around the world is an issue. Why does this player not do well at one club but does well at another? That to me is identification, coaching, maybe complementing philosophy as well, whatever it is. Having coached youth level, Ange has got an eye. It makes it easier for him to identify talent going to senior level – or from other parts of the world.

'So even look at someone like Aaron Mooy, whom he signed without much fanfare, I'd imagine, in Scotland. He's gone in and done really well, playing in a different role to what he's used to. I just know Ange will have looked at him, having known Aaron as a youth player, identified certain traits and said to himself: "In my philosophy, he can play the No.10 role pretty well. He'll do that for me." That's a really great quality for any manager to have, to be able to know – as much as anyone can – that a player is going to fit into his system and do a specific job.'

In an age when most clubs will have someone 'upstairs' asking questions about sell-on value, age profile and potential upsides versus the cost of a signing going wrong, it takes a strong character to continually back themselves in the market. Because anyone can spot a good player. Only a rare few can pick the guy who is definitely going to cope well with the change of environment, the noticeably quicker pace and notably less subtle physicality of Scottish or English football.

To hear Postecoglou talk about his record in an area of the game that can come to define a manager, however, it all seems strikingly simple. This is what we need. That guy provides it. We can afford him. Let's go.

'It comes to me having a real clear idea of how you want the game to be played,' he told Australian streaming service Stan, in an interview that covered recruitment.

'I've often said I could go into a shop with my wife, and she'll know exactly what to pick and buy. And mate, I've got no idea! When I go looking for players, I'm the same. I've got a real clear idea. When I see what I want, I picture them in my team – and when they fit that picture, most of the time it works.

'It comes back to the first thing; I have absolute clarity about how I want my team to play. What quality each player should have in each position. That should make it easier for the players as well, because they've already got some of the things I'm looking for, so their adjustment period becomes quicker.

'The players I've brought in [at Celtic] have hit the ground running and people ask why so quickly. But it's because I already know they've got the attributes I'm looking for – and the rest is just understanding the game plan.

'I knew that getting the right players was going to be the first critical part of what I am trying to create and how I will be judged in history. If I signed players that didn't fit, it was going to be hard. I wanted to make sure the players fitted the ideology of the team I wanted us to be. They also had to hit the right demographic in terms of ages. That was all-important.

'It's always been a big part of what I do. You can't have square pegs in round holes. It's not just about getting talented footballers, it's about getting people who fit into my football. A key one was Kyogo Furuhashi, who I knew from Japan. My team played against his and I watched him close up. I knew he had all the ingredients to be a success over here. As an individual player, but also because of the talent he had. I knew he would fit into my team.'

Postecoglou places as much emphasis on surrounding himself with good staff. Which has meant, with the odd exception, not taking his assistants with him when he moves club. Partly because they're usually ready to branch out on their own managerial adventure. But also because he loves the challenge of doing what he did at Celtic – walking into a boot room full of strange faces and converting them all to his way of thinking.

'If I'm going to have longevity in this game, I have to make sure my message stays relevant,' he explained, in a webinar for coaches during his time as Yokohama boss. 'So 20-something years ago when I won my first championship, I had a great message. If I stuck with that message today, the world is totally different. I need to evolve my ideas and beliefs. Bringing in new coaches forces me to make the message relevant.

'And it simplifies everything. If there is real clarity around what we want to do, then if you're suggesting something to me, if that doesn't fit into the way we want to play our game, I won't use it. I look for people who are brave and willing to go into the unknown, be willing to challenge themselves. I want people who don't see it as a job. It's not a job. If you're passionate and generally inquisitive, the knowledge will be there. If I see someone who is a little bit conservative and is happy just to have a job in football, that's not how I work. If you're not bold in your approach and you're not brave in these areas, you're not going to fit in with the programme I've set up. Whether you're a staff member or a player.

'When we're recruiting players or staff, the kind of person they are is very important, as well. If they are conservative in their nature or sort of set in their ways, it's going to be very hard – unless they're already playing this style of football – to convince them to play this way. Everything we do, in terms of sports science, recruitment, it all comes back to that desire to be an aggressive, bold, attacking team.'

Working within a modern football department, with scouts to manage and final decisions to make, is made easier, according to Postecoglou, by the way he briefs his talent spotters.

'We had real success with our recruitment because there was a real clarity about what we wanted,' he explained. 'We didn't just want a striker who scored goals. We wanted a striker who could play in a certain way. We didn't want a centre back who was just strong and good in the air, it was a specific type of centre back we were looking for. The reason I've had success in my career is that it is really clear to everybody.

'When I first started coaching, I was doing everything. I was the English model of a manager, doing all the transfers, the negotiations, even the contracts. At Yokohama I was pretty lucky there was a good system in place. I've worked with some great sporting directors and, of course, City Football Group [the people who run Yokohama, New York City and, of course, Manchester City] who have a tremendous scouting system for all the international markets. But all those systems are very dependent on having the clarity of what you want. The success or failure of any recruitment system is having a very clear idea of the kind of player you want, the kind of person you want.

'Whatever strategy you use, if you don't have clarity on how you want to play, it's going to cloud things. Because the world is full of fantastic footballers. How are you going to know which of those fantastic footballers is going to fit into your system?'

Chapter 9

ADVANCE AUSTRALIA FAIR

IT'S fair to say that Ange Postecoglou has a complicated relationship with Australian football, Aussie sport in general, the media Down Under . . . pretty much the entire country, truth be told. And that is only right. In an age when too many wrap themselves in this or that flag as a way of avoiding critical thinking, a healthy degree of scepticism should be an integral element of anyone's patriotism, with an acknowledgement of faults – institutional, cultural or individual – essential in guarding against the sort of hubristic exceptionalism that inevitably undermines the most noble of intentions.

Postecoglou's love of Australia has never been about pledging unthinking allegiance to the green and gold while making bold declarations of superiority. Nor, interestingly, has he ever succumbed to the sort of insecurity that has seemingly dogged every step forward taken by the Socceroos.

His is a higher kind of loyalty to the nation where he grew up, played all his football, and did most of his coaching. It is a love of a country requiring him to speak out against cack-handed mismanagement, doubt disguised as bravado – and a thousand other faults preventing Australia from getting fully behind 'soccer'. It is also an unyielding belief that, given the right support, the national team he coached with such distinction should be setting their sights far higher than merely qualifying for the World Cup Finals.

During his time as Socceroos boss from 2013 to 2017, he regularly found himself at odds with his employers, seemingly choking on the official-issue gag that prevented him from weighing in on matters of national performance; the discomfort of having to retract fairly even-handed comments on a 2015 dispute between players and Football Federation Australia certainly stuck in his craw, according to one confidant. Ultimately, he walked away from the job after guiding them through qualification for the 2018 Finals in Russia, not because he didn't fancy returning to the biggest event in global sport – but because he couldn't go along with a philosophy that settled for simply taking part in the tournament.

Slowly, the people who run the game Down Under have begun to come around to his way of thinking. Slowly. Now hailed as a great ambassador for the game, with friends and former colleagues joking that he could easily run for president of Australia, once The Republic is established in full, Postecoglou understands that his current status may be only fleeting. That it doesn't take much for the mob to turn against even the most popular of figures. Especially one with a penchant for telling inconvenient truths and issuing blunt reminders about the state of play back 'home'.

You must also remember that Ange is the product of a community not always afforded first-class treatment by their fellow Australians. Growing up in an environment where soccer was the 'foreign' sport, his efforts to establish

a team at Prahran High School met with a mix of indiffer-
ence and hostility in an age of open prejudice. As part of a
huge Greek diaspora, the largest outside of Cyprus, kids
with last names like Postecoglou, Maikousis and Dimitrakis
– speaking a different language at home, eating different
foods and even playing a really odd version of 'footy' – were
always at least half a step removed from the Anglo-Australian
mainstream. And, if the general attitude towards immigrants has slowly evolved over the decades, the media Down
Under still stand accused, on occasion, of treating the
world's most popular team sport with patronisingly passing
interest, at best. With the worst reserving complete disdain
for the game.

The critics deeply invested in protecting the AFL, in
particular, from encroaching on proper Aussie territory
have often been aided and abetted, bizarrely, by the game's
own lack of confidence in its own heritage, its rich history,
even its right to exist as a full member of Australia's sporting
story. How else do you explain the governing bodies'
repeated attempts to impose a sort of ethnic cleansing on its
elite competitions, with clubs put under direct and indirect
pressure to sweep away all those Hajduk, Hellas and
Juventus banners deemed unappetising to the floating
voters/new customers beloved by marketing men the world
over?

As recently as 2014, teams were forced to adopt
Australianised names under the hated – and frankly sinister
– National Club Identity Policy. The smallest flag on a
jersey had to be removed or, in one famous incident, taped
over before an FFA Cup tie. Melbourne Knights weren't
even allowed to have Melbourne Croatia social club as shirt

sponsors. All vestiges of history based on ethnicity or country of origin were to be erased. To put that in a UK context, just imagine if, as recently as a decade ago, the SFA had decided that it simply wouldn't do for certain clubs to carry on celebrating, or even acknowledging, their 'non-Scottish' roots. Sorry, Hibernian. Get rid of that harp and call yourself Edinburgh Greens. And Celtic? Well, take your pick of new names. Just don't make it too Irish . . .

The Aussie clubs founded by all those Italians, Greeks, Croats, Macedonians and the rest were forced to fall into line, at least for the five years it took someone at FIFA to overturn such a ridiculous policy. By that stage, of course, the old originals had already been robbed of their places on the national stage. Shoved back into regionalised ghettos, their places were taken by the homogenised 'franchises' of the A-League.

So, yeah, a Greek boy who grew up in Melbourne in the 1970s is allowed to feel a little conflicted about his dual nationality. Even if, like almost every kid who ever found themselves caught between two homelands, Postecoglou found a way to be part of both, somehow managing to commit himself to each without short-changing either. Even demonstrating that loyalty through national service.

A winner of just four international caps during his playing days, the future Socceroos boss was initially in the running to take over the senior team in 2000, not long after leading South Melbourne to the inaugural FIFA World Club Championship – but lost out to Frank Farina. Offered the under-20/under-17s role as a consolation prize, he leapt at the chance to make major changes – he hoped – in the development of young Australian internationals. He stayed for seven years, doing a lot of good work behind the scenes. Without getting back-up during a transformative time for the domestic game, with the lack of first-team exposure afforded young Aussie players by top-flight teams becoming an increasing source of frustration.

That first spell with the national federation ended, rather infamously, following that spectacular seven-minute televised argument with player-turned-pundit Craig Foster. But Ange himself always got the feeling that something less obvious than a PR disaster, or even a run of bad results, lay in the decision to let him go, writing in his own autobiography: 'I was seen as part of "old soccer"; a barnacle of the ethnic enclaves that bound the NSL [National Soccer League] together. Someone like me would only poison the new system because I was so inextricably linked with the old one . . . so, after seven years in the job as youth boss, doing what I now call my PhD in coaching, I was released. All the knowledge I'd accumulated was just expunged.'

This railing against football's 'scorched earth reflex' is something of a favourite theme for Postecoglou, who believes the game should be far better at tapping into the knowledge and experience of those who have been doing good work. He is also fiercely proud of Australian football's many achievements, whether that be exporting a golden generation of players to European clubs – something that he traces back to the famous Australian Institute of Sport model copied by countries all over the world – or the Socceroos harnessing all of that talent to come within one dodgy penalty of reaching the 2006 World Cup quarter-finals.

Although always open to new ideas, a 2004 visit to the much-admired French Football Federation talent factory at

Clairefontaine left Postecoglou convinced that no country possesses all the secrets to identifying and nurturing the next generation of talented footballers. And that the greatest indicators can often be revealed to the astute observer simply through doing the job for long enough. He was never one of those calling for European ideas and models to be imported, wholesale, to the Australian game.

If you want to really wind him up, meanwhile, ask about the regular stream of patronising quotes trotted out by European players signed by Australian clubs, particularly all their pat statements about being really impressed with the standard of play. He cringes at this constant need for external validation. And understands that, unless based on an honest assessment, warts and all, this sort of praise is absolutely worthless. Scots weary of hearing pundits forever seeking to have our 'wee league' given the approval by some marquee signing – or, worse, the Manchester United/Liverpool/Arsenal academy kid embarking on their first loan spell to the Badlands of the SPFL – understood exactly where he was coming from.

Possibly even more galling to Postecoglou has been Australian football's inability to capitalise on his successful spell as Socceroos coach. Appointed in 2013 following the departure of German coach Holger Osieck, he inherited a team who had qualified for the 2014 World Cup in Brazil. But an ageing squad too reliant on past glories. A team who had just suffered back-to-back humiliations, in the shape of 6–0 friendly losses to both France and Brazil, the quality of the opposition doing little to quell the backlash that eventually cost Osieck his position.

Under Ange's guidance, the Aussies didn't manage to win a game in Brazil. But they did perform with credit against

Chile, the Netherlands and Spain. Far more tangible success quickly followed under the new manager's guidance, with victory in the 2015 Asian Cup still regarded as one of the finest achievements in the history of Australian sport. Partly because of the excitement generated by hosting – and then winning – the tournament over 23 days in January, with sold-out stadia and wall-to-wall media coverage offering a glimpse of just how big soccer might become, should Australia's status as the Land of the Fair Go prove more than just a trite slogan. Despite leading them to success in the World Cup qualifying campaign that followed, however, Postecoglou wasn't happy. Couldn't be satisfied working for people who refused to see the bigger picture – a grand vista involving the Socceroos becoming not just a regional power-house, but a force in world football.

Reluctant to discuss the exact reasons behind his departure for a long time, Postecoglou eventually opened up in an interview with the *Herald Sun* a couple of years after the event, explaining: 'It was a generational change; the greats were getting to the end. There was a real opportunity with a new group to grow and try something different as a nation, with the way we play and do things.

'That got chipped away. In the end, people made it very clear that all they were interested in was whether we'll qualify. Nothing else mattered. At that point I thought: "OK, let's qualify and then I can go off and do things again that were challenging for me."

'What was driving me was trying to create something. I knew it was going to be a tough ask to marry this idyllic view of how I wanted us to play football with the harsh reality of results. But I was confident I could do it. In the end, I was the only one thinking that way. FFA weren't. The board wasn't. And it's their right. They thought: "Great, fantastic, nice words. But we just want to qualify for the World Cup because, if we don't, it's a disaster for the game."'

More recently, in a 2022 interview with Aussie TV station Stan Sport, he put a little more meat on the bone in explaining his general unease about being allowed the freedom needed to transform the Socceroos, saying: 'The reason I was obsessed with winning the Asian Cup was because I thought that could be a watershed moment for Australian football – because I think winning is everything. I equated it to the Euros. When a nation wins the Euros, irrespective of how strong a nation – could be a Denmark or Greece – it's a seminal moment in that country's evolution because, all of a sudden, they feel like they've achieved something.

'I thought [that] would then give me the power and also allow me the opportunity and us as a nation to stand up and say: "OK, this is who we are now." I wanted us to be the Brazil or the Germany [of Asia] . . . and that was my starting point. I misread what happened, what the impact it would possibly have. Then through that [Russia] World Cup campaign, I felt we'd just gone back into that cycle again of not understanding what it takes to become a really strong footballing nation. It wasn't just about qualifying for World Cups, it was about having an identity, believing in something.

'That was going to be my benchmark – from now on, don't accept anything less than winning the Asian Cup every time, qualifying for the World Cup and being the number one nation in Asia. And I couldn't find that golden key to open that up.'

As ever, he gives the impression of a man – a visionary man, but mortal all the same – butting heads with a solid wall of bricks comprised of 51 per cent pragmatism and 49 per cent fear. He was imagining where Australia might go, as a football nation. While the body responsible for the game, its sustainability and its ability to remain relevant were reluctant to put qualification at risk. In a country raised on a diet of international success in cricket and rugby (both codes), the Socceroos not even securing a place in the World Cup would inevitably generate a firestorm of criticism and negativity, all gleefully supported by influential media figures looking to give football a kicking.

Chris Nikou, the current president of Football Federation Australia, was on the board back when all of this happened. He understood the pressure to play safe. And could see where Ange was coming from. They had been friends, after all, since childhood; when we spoke in early 2023, Nikou made it an easy 45 years since they first met.

Offering his own take on how things played out when Postecoglou walked away from a team he'd just guided to the 2018 Finals, Nikou said simply: 'His one KPI [key performance indicator] was to get the Socceroos qualified. He was the first Aussie coach, really, to do it. Because we had Holger Osieck, Pim Verbeek and Guus Hiddink do it before then.

'With Ange, he'd already had the experience of coaching at the Brazil World Cup. Maybe if he hadn't already been to the tournament, he might not have left. I've not asked him that. But he's always wanted to challenge himself, which is why he went to Japan, why he went to Celtic. At that time

[2017], it was a difficult campaign. And, despite all the various odds for us and the continental play-off, he got them qualified. That's all we could ask.

'He had taken over just before the Brazil World Cup and had to make a critical analysis of what he had, with one eye on the Asian Cup which was being hosted by Australia the following January. I think he got the best out of the players, although there were players who probably peaked during that tournament. I genuinely think he wanted a fresh challenge.

'Now, if you go back to what happened with the young Socceroos, I think it was very unfair that the ills of the pathways were blamed on Ange. Because he's a bloody good coach. Maybe not a magician. Not far off it. But, because they didn't qualify [for the 2007 FIFA Youth World Cup Finals], you blame the coach. I don't think there's much more he could have done with that squad. Our pathways are the subject of a different discussion down here. We don't get the minutes into our younger players that Scottish football does, for instance, because we simply don't have enough teams or enough games. Our domestic competition, the A-League, is only 27 games. Compare that to 38 games in Scotland plus two cup competitions, maybe Europe. So you get the minutes for players there.

'Ange could have just thrown the towel in after what happened to him. But I think we're all so glad he stuck at it. We inducted him into the Hall of Fame last year, so that tells you something about how we value him. He was a very good player, had success as a player, he was a captain, so that tells you about his leadership. But his coaching is what stands out. And a lot of players he coached have gone into coaching themselves; Kevin Muscat took over at Yokohama – he's a prime example. But there are others. He took Harry Kewell into the Celtic set-up and that's going to be a real benefit to Harry, we all know that. He has experience of coaching at a World Cup – and the experience of then qualifying for a World Cup, which is never easy down here, because we've got to go through the Asian qualification, which has its own difficulties. But Ange's influence has been the way football is played, the way he believes it should be played, to entertain.'

It's never just about entertaining, of course. As we've learned by now, Postecoglou builds teams capable of playing expansive football because he believes it's the only way to compete against the very best. You'd think that, in a country occasionally given reason to believe itself the greatest sporting nation on earth, pitching that sort of ambitious blueprint would be an easy sell. Peter Filopoulos, another long-term Postecoglou friend and colleague who is now head of marketing at Football Federation Australia, is quicker to concede that Ange was on to something with his constant demands for not merely greater ambition but more investment – and a more typically Aussie heads-high, chests-out brashness when it comes to fighting football's corner.

'He's right,' said Filopoulos. 'We're slowly winning that battle. It's nowhere near where it was when he was coaching domestically here; it's a lot better. We've got a long, long journey ahead. And a lot of it's got to do with the fact that the NRL and the AFL have got a stronghold on the biggest tabloids. They control the narrative.

'But I think we're winning. We're winning the grassroots

battle. We're the number one sport, participation wise, from the age group of 14 to 24; the interest in football is three times that of the NRL [rugby league] and twice that of the AFL. So, I think it's evolving and the culture – and we're growing. We're the only sport in Australia that is growing at the rate it's growing participation wise, and we're starting to produce talent. We're doing well on the world stage. And our Matildas and our Socceroos now occupy two of the top three spots in national team favouritism – and we've got a Women's World Cup on our doorstep. It's starting to change; the big bus is turning.

'When you look at what Ange is doing now, that can only help. He's given our country hope that a guy like Ange Postecoglou, born in Athens and emigrated to Australia with his family as a young boy, played football all his life, you know, in the local community, can end up coaching one of the biggest football brands in the world. There's a pathway for you right at the top level of Australian football, but also with the rest of the world. I really believe that.'

Given near-universal approval ratings for Postecoglou and a general air of optimism around Australian football, helped by the Socceroos only just losing out to eventual champions Argentina in the last 16 at the 2022 World Cup in Qatar, there are some obvious questions about how the federation couldn't find a way to hang on to a coach who was only asking for a bit of time and understanding. What could possibly have driven Ange away from such a prestigious job?

Intriguingly, Filopoulos goes back to an incident in September 2015, two years before Postecoglou's departure, when the head coach found himself caught in the middle of a labour dispute between players and his employers – and let rip in public, criticising both sides for allowing their arguments to overshadow a crucial World Cup qualifier. He was merely venting his frustration over an argument that saw several Socceroos boycott commercial appearances in Perth. He wasn't taking sides. And that was the problem.

Within hours, the governing body had put out a retraction that read like one of those scripted hostage statements, the head coach quoted as saying: 'As a senior employee of Football Federation Australia [FFA] I understand that my comments were inappropriate. I appreciate that I need to take sides on this issue. The commercial performance of the Socceroos brand directly affects the amount of investment in the match schedule, technical developments and sports science staff.

'In this case, the commercial boycotts imposed by Professional Footballers Australia [PFA] will directly affect commercial partners and will inevitably hurt the Socceroos program.

'I made comments yesterday out of frustration. I acknowledge that the PFA initiated the regrettable situation that has distracted us in Perth. I understand that FFA was compelled to respond in order to explain its position to the game's stakeholders. I call on the PFA to undertake that no future Socceroo camp will be targeted in this way.'

Right. There's quite a lot to unpack in that collection of corporately approved words definitely said/written by the man himself. Not only was he forced into a climbdown but made to put his name to a statement critical of the very same players he'd now be expected to lead through a typically arduous qualification campaign. You can see why Filopoulos harked back to this incident when our conversation, on a quiet Melbourne afternoon, turned to the complex mosaic of reasons behind the manager's decision to stand down.

Taking up the story, he said: 'I recall we were in Perth and there was a big CBA [collective bargaining agreement] discussion with the PFA [the footballers' union] – and it wasn't going well; there was a bit of a war of words in the papers, right before a qualifier.

'And in a press conference, Ange was asked: "Ange, what are your thoughts on this?" And he came out and pretty much honestly said: "I would have thought that this topic could have been parked in the lead-up to the World Cup qualifiers, at least publicly. And then we can just be mature enough as a sport to park it, get through this World Cup qualification, and we'll pick up the conversation because it's distracting my camp."

'And the CEO at the time publicly whacked him and told him he needed to know his place, and he shouldn't have said that. To me, that moment was the moment that began the demise of his relationship with the federation. He won't say it. But I know Ange. I also don't think there was enough support around what he wanted to do. He's got a strong philosophy, what he wants to do, how he wants to go about it. I don't think there was enough support.'

Now free to share his thoughts on Aussie soccer without fear of anyone – up to and including the prime minister, quite probably – telling him to wind his neck in, Postecoglou continues to act as a long-distance agitator for change in the way his country treats football.

When the boys in the gold shirts made the knockout stages in Qatar, for instance, there were wild scenes of celebration in the wee small hours back home, with the footage from Melbourne's Federation Square generating global coverage, while even the Aussie Rules-dominated media were putting the Socceroos top of the bill, leading bulletins while dominating the back pages. For a few days, at least, anything seemed possible.

Yet Postecoglou was quick to add a warning into his genuinely heartfelt words of congratulation, pointing out: 'We've done that in the past – and it usually takes a week before the headlines change. The challenge for the sport is to capitalise on the impact these guys have made. Unfortunately, in the past it's been about missed opportunities. I'm hoping the lessons have been learned.

'It's about getting support from the government and being treated like a top-tier sport, like the other codes are. The reality is the other codes are not international sports. Football is the one that brings the world's attention to Australia. The people who have the purse strings need to understand that and what they have seen this week is the tip of the iceberg if they back the sport.

'They need to see those scenes at 3 a.m. in Melbourne. It's not just about football becoming stronger, it's about Australia being stronger as a nation.'

That vision of a stronger Australia, in footballing terms, possibly involves a few difficult conversations. Perhaps even an apology or two. They could do worse, of course, than to seek advice from a figure whose success in Japan and Scotland has given him a special status in Aussie sport. One that would almost certainly have seemed improbable, maybe even impossible, to the little Greek boy growing up in Prahran.

Nick Galatas, the former South Melbourne chairman who has campaigned for a return of the old 'ethnic' clubs to a new national competition, said of Postecoglou's place in the nation's affections: 'There is massive, massive pride. That's undeniable. Across the board, it has transcended the Greek community. He is Australian, an Australian guy, and I love to see he has been a unifying force, not intentionally, just by doing what he does; he brought the game together.

'For those people, for those of us . . . I grew up in the same era he did, our generation of people, and those who came a bit before and a bit after, we see that as one of us has risen. And all of Australia feels like that, in a way. If you're Welsh and you see Ryan Giggs at Manchester United or Gareth Bale winning the Champions League, you embrace that. I mean, I don't know what the Liberians thought of George Weah . . . But, yeah, I reckon Ange could be president! When we have our republic finally!'

Former Socceroos captain Paul Wade, widely regarded as one of the greatest players ever to represent the country, was equally enthusiastic when we spoke about Postecoglou's influence on the game back home – and the unyielding philosophy needed to transform a country previously content with a place on soccer's sidelines.

'He's so forward-thinking,' said Wade, who won 84 full caps in a career that totalled 118 international appearances, including Olympic fixtures. 'We had a guy called Frank Arok who coached the Socceroos. And he said losing 1-0 wasn't good enough any more. It changed things. That was the start of making players believe something. Ange now does a job in making us believe that getting to the round of

16 isn't good enough. He's dragging us into the 21st century. Some are happy with what we've got. Not Ange.

'I do leadership talks and we all use some of the comments Ange makes. He brings, however, many thousands of people together to believe one thing; it's such a pleasure to see. We've never seen an Australian coach at that level before. To see it now, to see it being done the way it is, educating people who thought they knew everything, is amazing. We're just so proud of what he's doing.'

Amid the flag waving and sense of national pride in watching one of their own do well in Europe, there must surely be a few bright sparks in Australian football still scratching their heads – or grinding their teeth – over the national team ever letting this guy get on that flight to Japan.

'I think all of Australia regrets not having him along for longer,' is how long-time assistant Peter Cklamovski puts it. 'I think that's fair to say. It would've been great to go to a World Cup, another World Cup, with him. I think the team were primed for it, hungry for it. Everybody there believed in what we were doing in camp. Football can be a bit funny sometimes, what you wish would happen some- times doesn't and then you just sort of go separate ways.'

There is, of course, a great irony in the fact that Ange Postecoglou had to go to Japan, Scotland and now England in order to not merely enhance his own reputation, in a global sense, but prove Australia's mettle as a footballing nation. Not all heroes wear an FFA tracksuit, right?

A genuine sports nut who loves his AFL, rugby, cricket and all the rest, Postecoglou will always fight the corner for his country. And for his game. That's where the conflict arises.

Speaking to the same Craig Foster whose belligerent line of questioning caused his first split from Football Federation Australia, the pair now reconciled and united by a shared interest in improving the treatment of refugees, Postecoglou made an interesting observation about the way football is still viewed back home.

'I talk to so many of our greatest footballers who live overseas permanently,' he said, adding: 'Part of their disenchantment, I know, is when they dipped their toe back in Australia, it wasn't as welcoming a place – in a football sense – as it might have been. I'm the first cab on the rank, in terms of being the oldest, and hopefully people are more receptive in future. But there's no guarantee of that.'

In other words, it's complicated. Always has been.

Key Game

AUSTRALIA 2 SOUTH KOREA 1

Asian Cup Final
31 January 2015

LOOKING back on this now, Postecoglou considers this career high point – a masterpiece of coaching, to quote one member of the Socceroos staff – as something of a missed opportunity. Always thinking of the bigger picture, he believed that a major tournament victory, a triumph on home soil that captured the imagination of the Australian public, would establish the Socceroos as a genuine force in Asian football. On a personal level, then, he sees the aftermath of victory at Sydney's Stadium Australia as a time when his discontent – the unease over Football Australia's lack of ambition that would lead to him leaving the national team after qualifying for the 2018 World Cup – began to take root.

In the heat of the moment, though? Well, anyone who couldn't enjoy the drama and joy of a thrilling extra-time victory needed to find a different career path. This was as good as football gets. And as influential a coaching performance as many can remember.

The bare facts show that Australia, who had lost narrowly to South Korea in the group stages, were 1–0 up heading into injury time of the final. When Son Heung-min scored to equalise with the 90 minutes up and the frenzied home crowd clamouring for the final whistle, well, it was a staggering blow to the Socceroos. But not, thanks to

Postecoglou's grasp on both the bigger picture and the granular details, a knockout punch.

The manager had worked a recurring theme into almost every team talk, training session and analysis briefing over the months leading up to the tournament, emphasising the opportunity these players had to write their own special chapter in Australian football. He'd prepared them for that challenge by, in the wake of the 2014 World Cup, arranging a whole slew of testing friendly internationals away from home, spending 'six months on the road', as he put it, in order to make his players mentally resilient. On top of that, the team's sports science expert – Dr Craig Duncan – had become central to everything, not just for the advice he provided, but for the way he'd constantly remind players of just how strong they were. The fittest in the tournament. They knew that for a fact. And Doc Duncan could quote the numbers to back it up.

Now, in this moment of crisis, Postecoglou would return to both the wider narrative and the simple facts of the situation. With one of the shortest speeches of his career.

In the brief interlude between full time and extra time, the manager – wrestling with his own disappointment but taking himself away from the group to gather his thoughts, finding some solitude in a stadium of 80,000 souls – saw the South Korean players slumped on the turf as they took on board fluid and information. Turning round, hoping to God that his Socceroos wouldn't be in the same state of physical and mental exhaustion, he saw them standing tall and proud, some even refusing offers of water. They were ready. They would do this. He just had to tell them as much.

In his autobiography, *Changing the Game*, he recalled having just 30 seconds to influence what would happen next. Gathering the group around and telling them to look across at their opponents sprawling on the pitch, he told them: 'They're on the ground. Everything we've spoken about for six months since the World Cup has led to this moment. We're stronger, we're fitter. Craig's been telling you and now you can see it for yourselves. We have more belief than they do because we know what we set out for. That hasn't changed one bit and it's now very close to happening. You've worked every minute of the last 30 days for this moment and you're ready for it. You will win. And you'll make that chapter on the Asian Cup even more memorable.'

Postecoglou's assistant with Australia, Peter Cklamovski, believes the emotional intelligence shown by his friend and mentor before and during the Asian Cup adventure is what sets him apart. Nothing he did was by chance. And, for someone so famously taciturn even when dealing with close colleagues, he wasn't afraid to give others a freedom to really open up. Which is why, in the training camp before the Asian Cup kicked off, the boss asked each player to stand up, in front of the group, and tell their story. Explain how they started playing football, pay tribute to the parents who maybe scrimped and saved to buy boots or take them to a tournament, reveal a little of what it meant to be an international footballer. It was, according to those in the room at the time, a deeply moving session.

Cklamovski, recalling how his gaffer had deliberately engineered this sort of scenario in order to create a feeling of kinship among a group who would all have very different experiences, in terms of playing time, highs, lows, good days and bad days, over the course of the tournament, said simply: 'It was the masterpiece of Ange's work. It was around 35 days in camp before the Asian Cup, that's preparation time, then, of course, it's tournament mode. I just felt like it was a masterpiece of Ange's work, the way he delivered messages every day, how he constructed the team identity and the purpose of the group. And everyone talks about the Asian Cup final as a big game and a pivotal moment. For sure, it's the trophy game, but there were many times during the tournament when I just knew we were going to win it. There was something in me. I felt it, I knew it.

'There was a ten-month period under Ange where we didn't win a game. That was before the Asian Cup. This is why I say it's a masterpiece, because Ange chose to play as many away games as possible which potentially could help the group with travel. We played some big tough games: Belgium away, Germany away – twice, Japan away. It was a really good patch of games for us as a national team, but without a win for ten months. That was leading up to the Asian Cup. It was part of his master plan. When we got into the Asian Cup, we were on our home soil, the momentum was there to do something special, and away we went. Everyone talks about the Asian Cup final, but there was a big piece of work that goes into that, and everything connected to that moment. That was an example of what made Ange such an exceptional leader, character and coach.'

Chapter 10

NO MAN IS AN ISLAND, BUT ISTHMUS COME CLOSE

TALES of Ange Postecoglou's cold-eyed, cold-hearted, cold shoulder approach when dealing with players and fellow coaches have taken on an almost legendary quality. Which is kind of what he wants, right? All part of the plan for someone who understands the value of placing barriers between himself and the people he's expected to lead, without fear or favour. This is a man who recognises the importance of standing apart from those whose fate he holds in his hands. Puts great stock in being seen as anything but one of the lads. He is the authority figure whose final word might as well be carved in stone. So, yeah, he's quietly content with the exaggerations and over-spun stories about him blanking senior members of his own Socceroos squad, walking past star performers in hallways without so much as a nod, refusing all invitations to socialise with staff – or generating such an unease that, back in his A-League days, players used to fight with each other to avoid sitting next to him on flights across Australia. This is a guy who, last season, answered a question about keeping Celtic's fringe players happy by saying: 'I laugh when I get asked this. What am I supposed to do, be making them cups of tea and sending flowers to their wives?' Clearly, there's a point to being regarded, by one and all, as the biggest, baddest, most unyielding character in the room.

But there is, of course, another side to Postecoglou. A man several evolutionary steps removed from old-fashioned ideas about managers as martinets, barking out orders with God-like authority and demanding – always demanding – strict obedience from the minions employed to do their bidding. For starters, there is the close circle of friends who speak so readily and glowingly about his warmth. Plus the countless good turns he's done young coaches making their way in the game, growing into his role as mentor and adviser. He also understands that modern players won't respond to the outdated ideas that, right up until the early 2000s, saw even certain Premier League clubs treat injured players as malingerers, leaving the treatment room ice-cold to increase discomfort and scheduling appointments to coincide with rush-hour traffic.

But, most importantly, any character study of Postecoglou must also factor in the surprising professional support network he's built outside of football.

'AA for coaches' is how the man himself describes the monthly Zoom meetings of elite leaders, legendary rugby coach Eddie Jones among them, who enjoy spending the odd hour moaning to each other about the daily frustrations of their chosen profession. As the man who set up this great meeting of minds puts it, there is no great difference between leading a national rugby team into a World Cup, guiding an AFL squad through the play-offs or trying to get Celtic into the Champions League. It is all, as they suggest, 'the same shit in a different bucket'. God, if you don't harbour even a grudging admiration for the seemingly innate Aussie ability to bastardise the 'Queen's Own English' with consistent wit and invention, there's something wrong with you.

It must also be pointed out that Postecoglou is acutely aware of the price he's paid for deliberately shutting himself off from his staff, writing in his autobiography about how much he would have loved to spend those long nights before an away game grabbing a burger and beer with his fellow coaches, instead of locked up in his room eating room service and watching another rerun of *M*A*S*H*. He acknowledges that, in terms of enriching life experiences, he would have benefited enormously from simply opening up and getting to know people better.

But this is the philosophy he has chosen to pursue. It's the way things have to be. Which is why the legend has perhaps grown a few arms, legs, tails and heads over the years, with almost everyone interviewed for this book providing some example of Ange leaving an underling wondering what on earth he'd done to annoy the gaffer. One particularly oft-repeated favourite involves an assistant coach, after almost two weeks away in camp with the Young Socceroos, approaching the team manager to ask why Postecoglou hadn't said a word to him, only to be told: 'Oh, mate, you're fine. It's when he asks to talk to you, that's when you should be worried . . .'

From countless conversations over months of research, it's equally clear that Postecoglou's no-nonsense approach has limits. Players with personal issues know that he will help in any way he can. Those players also know that he is deeply invested in their success as individuals. They just don't expect him to show it all that often.

When he does open up, it's to people he considers his peers. High-performance coaches and managers who can understand exactly what he's going through. Content to admit that he can be one of the world's great grumps, when things don't go his way, he admits that he's really benefited from those monthly Zooms – far more than merely opportunities to vent. The knowledge exchanged, criticisms accepted and reassurances received during any such meeting of minds are as valuable as gold to any coach.

In this particular instance, you'd also put good money on the chat occasionally veering towards the uproarious. Oh, to have been a fly on the virtual wall as Jones held forth on exactly why Ange should lob a few verbal hand grenades at the opposition ahead of the next derby at Ibrox or Celtic Park. What? You just know Eddie has suggested exactly that, at some point.

These think tank-style summits were first organised on behalf of a friend of a friend who runs a company called Aleda. Ironically enough, that name is derived from the old Scots word *alede*, which means to guide or to teach. There's plenty of that going on when characters from rugby, basketball, AFL, football and other sports get together. So successful has the first collective been that any number of world-class coaches, Mikel Arteta among them, are now lining up to seek their own version of sporting group therapy.

Tim Schleiger, the old Postecoglou pal who now specialises in sports science and conditioning, explained the thinking behind the concept he helped to implement, saying: 'Ange wasn't going to open up to Steven Gerrard when he's the gaffer at Rangers, you know what I mean? Most gaffers, regardless of whether it's the round-ball game or cricket or

AFL, most coaches – head coaches, in particular – will talk about loneliness.

'But all of a sudden, you're put in a situation where you can share these stories with other coaches. They're all dealing with the same shit. Still managing characters and personalities. Still managing wanting to win. Still managing a board. Still managing supporters.

'My really good friend, Luke Darcy, who is an ex-Western Bulldogs captain in the AFL – a very, very impressive man – spoke to me about who we could get involved. He had this great business called Aleda. Initially they did a lot of professional personal growth; management strategies; leadership in business and the corporate world. When Luke joined as an ex-player, it was to bring some sports insight to the business. But then there was this idea that they'd put together a group of five or six different coaches from different sports. I had this great memory of Ange being an enormous sport lover. So he was a natural fit.

'We'd done the first one which included Justin Langer, who was the Australian cricket coach, and a few others. Basically, they spent six weeks together – it was a two hours a week commitment – and Luke is pretty good at getting them to feel a bit vulnerable, to discuss where they're at. And then obviously once they've got the trust in each other . . .

'Ange has described it as "AA for coaches". You've got a support group that you've got complete trust in. Everyone understands you because they're all walking the same journey, and you can open up and talk to those guys. And debrief and give advice.'

Schleiger admits that even he was slightly wary of approaching Postecoglou, repeating a familiar phrase among even old acquaintances: 'I don't like to bother him too much.' So, like all good consultants, he got someone else to do it. Vince Grella, the former Socceroos player whose agency had worked with Postecoglou, was the go-between.

'I was chatting to Vince one night, and Vinnie's a real old-school No.6 who just calls it as it is,' said Schleiger. 'So, I said: "Hey, man, I heard you're catching up with Ange next week?" I give him all the blah, blah, blah. I know him because of our relationship. And then I said: "I need you to have a chat with him about Aleda. I know Ange loves sport, and I know because he values professional development so greatly, he'll fucking love this. So, I need you to get him on board."

'Vinnie wasn't keen at first. He goes: "Ah, fucking hell, Schleigs. I don't want to talk about this!" But I said: "Nah, I need you to do this; it's gonna be a real game changer for him." And, so, he got on board.

'You see, one of the things I always remembered about Ange was how much he loved sport. Even as a Greek growing up in AFL territory, a lot of them get frustrated with soccer being second tier to AFL in this country and it's got to fight for its rights against basketball and other sports – as opposed to in Europe. But Ange loved those sports.

'Luke had called me and said: "We've got Eddie Jones, we've got Neil Craig who's an ex-AFL great. Luke's on the board at the Western Bulldogs so they've got Luke Beveridge, who's the Bulldogs coach. Do you reckon Ange would do it?" Because they had just started to make some waves, right away, I said: "Aw, mate, he'll love that because he loves sport."

'Brian Goorjian, a very famous American-born Australian basketball coach who coached the Australian basketball team to the bronze medal at the 2020 Olympics, was another suggestion. I called Brian straight away, and he was on board immediately.

'I know Neil Craig and Eddie Jones have been over to a couple of [Celtic] games and had a few whiskies with Ange. And Brian, I have a real regular dialogue with Brian, and I just remember him talking on Skype. You know what the Americans are like: "*Man*, I spoke to fucking Ange last night and that guy is a fucking *stud*. You know, the best thing about this is all of a sudden, I take an interest in other sports. Like, last night I even watched the Celtics play the Rangers!" I had to say to him: "Brian, it's not plural. It's Celtic. And it's Rangers. It's not Boston's basketball team versus New York's ice hockey team." '

Schleiger tells an enlightening story about Goorjian taking a specific man management problem to the group after his Boomers – the nickname for the Australian men's basketball team – had lost to the US Dream Team in the semi-finals at the Olympics. Needing to strike the right tone ahead of the bronze medal match, he wondered whether he should throw an arm around the group or, in his own words, 'smash them'. Imagine asking a brains trust involving Eddie Jones and Ange Postecoglou that question. Smashing duly occurred. And the bronze medal was claimed. It was always Goorjian's intent to challenge his players. He just needed a bit of reassurance. Back-up from 'the boys'.

Schleiger, bringing the conversation back to what Postecoglou has taken from – and added to – the group, said: 'I was over for a game last year and, you know, when I walked into the Celtic boardroom with a few others, I looked across and asked how he was enjoying the leadership stuff. He just said: "Mate, it's so good."

'The remarkable thing is, from that group now – that was the second group – things have grown. Mikel Arteta's in one, we've got a Green Bay Packers coach, the Collingwood [AFL] coach. And I remember Harry Kewell saying it'd be really good for him, just because he's got to adjust from his player mentality to a coaching mentality. People are banging on the door to be involved. Ange was ahead of the game. Again.'

There are people in football, as in all walks of life, who really make you think about the old Italian proverb that translates as something like: 'Everybody's friend is nobody's friend.' You know the types. Always scanning the room for the most important person, forever looking to press the flesh with someone who might be able to help them advance their own interests, whether that's greasing the wheels of a transfer or conjuring up a job offer – real or not quite kosher – that might be used to negotiate an improved contract *in situ*. Aggressive networkers, you might call them.

Now, Postecoglou has never been slow to spot the next big chance. And he's done the whole 'punditry as a way of reminding clubs that he's still alive' shuffle favoured by many an out-of-work manager. If he was never going to stay at Celtic when Spurs came calling, however, he managed to always avoid the impression of someone biding his time in Glasgow until something better came along.

Old friend Nick Deligiannis, obviously biased in his outlook, points out: 'He's had rocky times. And you'll know about them, right? But through all of that, he's always had the respect of everyone – because he's such a fantastic football person. He's had success, largely, so he has that respect.

But he's also a really humble person. You see it even now, when people are throwing all these accolades at him. He puts it in perspective.

'He's like a humble champion. And I reckon that's the best kind of champion. That's also why, to my mind, Celtic people took to him, because he's that kind of person. They love him as a character as much as what he's achieving, results wise.

'I think, with Ange, he's a very private person. He's so focused on what he does. But there's a group of four or five mates who are like his family. Beyond that, he talks to a lot of people, because in football you do that. But he's always got the people he trusts, the people closest to him, those he trusts unconditionally. He's a really loyal guy. He's part of a group of mates who would do anything for each other. He will say: "I don't care if I have anyone else as a mate – I'm perfectly happy with this small core!"

'And he keeps his distance from his players and staff – because he's always felt it's a tough enough job. You need distance to do the things you want to do, he believes. But he's also conscious that his job is to help people be their best. The balance of that, he's very good at separating that, very good at keeping his distance.

'He also, and I've seen this over time, has become something of a statesman in football circles over here. He's someone whom aspiring coaches look up to. And I think he gets a lot out of giving them a call along the way, giving them help if they reach out. He really enjoys that he's able to help others.'

The man himself expects no great credit for spending time talking to young coaches, sounding genuinely dismissive of the gratitude they express for something that comes naturally to him, saying: 'I've been doing this for a long time now. It's my 26th/27th year of managing at this level and, especially young coaches, if I can have any kind of chats with them and just give them a little bit of guidance, mainly the advice is just to be themselves. Particularly when you are a young manager, there are a lot of people telling you what to do and how to do things.

'I don't feel a loneliness in the job. I don't feel lonely. I've never felt isolated. I've loved what I have done. All of us have family and friends around us who can be that support network that you need.

'Aside from that, I think there is a general respect that all managers have for each other and an understanding for each other. We all feel for guys who are going through a tough time in our roles because we know that could be us one day. So there is a respect there.'

The thing that strikes most people as odd, when it comes to Postecoglou's insistence on standing slightly apart – or above – the group, is that he's also managed to keep people onside. At Celtic, he famously agreed to take on the existing backroom staff as part of the deal. Which meant walking into a room and convincing these guys to follow him. Without turning on the charm, schmoozing the dominant personality, making Brendan Rodgers-esque levels of eye contact and pretending to be their new best pal. How does that even work?

'I think he's an easy man to follow,' is how long-time assistant Peter Cklamovski answers that question, adding: 'a) because he's inspirational; and b) he's just an absolute gentleman. It's important for players and staff to believe in him, and that's what he mentioned when he started at

Celtic. That's not a hard thing to do, because it's Ange. Why I say that is because he's got clarity in what he wants on the pitch, how he wants his team to play and how that looks from a day-to-day perspective. That becomes very clear to follow, and to unify, and to progress.

'He's a genuine guy, so no one wants to let him down. And within all of that, there's a responsibility as a staff member to be the best in your area, the best in your field – whether you're assistant manager or team masseur – be the best in the country, be the best in the world at that. That's the mentality he sets up in the environment.

'I guess sometimes he chooses to be distant – that's well documented and he's got his reasons – and I think with that, he chooses where his energy can go. And maybe he just doesn't enjoy company sometimes!

'I think what's important was always himself. I don't know how he feels, genuinely, about missing a burger or missing a beer or anything. I can guarantee I wasn't having any beers or burgers with the staff around; I was working non-stop for him. He didn't stop thinking about how to build success in the project. But I guess everyone is different. That's the key to him – he will continue to do it his way. To be a great manager, you have to be comfortable doing it your way and being your own man.

'I actually started with Ange in 2004; that was preparation for the FIFA Under-17 World Championship. It was late 2004, and we were in Argentina for a month. I remember him being an absolute gentleman, first and foremost. And a great leader. To be fair, I was raw, and a young coach wanting to be the best support possible. A real gentleman but, importantly, a really good coach. That was under-17s and the level of, well, we were working with teenagers really, but I just looked at him and thought: "What a coach." The way he wants to play, how he set up the environment, what standards he had. He just resonated with me.

'At that point in my career, I was raw and hungry, and wanted to learn as much as I could – I was a sponge. Obviously, in camp mode, you're in each other's pocket. We had some really good times. The late, great Martyn Crook was a good friend of Ange's, his assistant and goal-keeping coach at the time. We had some special days – but all based on hard work and football.'

Players have always been made to understand that, in the long list of priorities dictating Postecoglou's decision-making, their feelings come very near the bottom, with former Celtic and Socceroos striker Scott McDonald – famously dropped to the bench, as national team captain for a World Cup glamour clash against Brazil – speaking from bitter experience when he explained: 'If he doesn't like you or need you, he doesn't give you an excuse or explana-tion. He doesn't need to. He's moving on. That's the way he works and you've got to respect that.

'I had been captain of his under-20s and was his most experienced campaigner, my third campaign in these World Cups. He pulled me into his hotel room before we played Brazil and we needed a result to go through to the next round – and he just said: "You're not playing. You don't suit the style of what we need to beat this team." He did what he thought was best and made the hard call.'

At club level, even those who felt Postecoglou always had their best interests at heart admit to finding him cold and distant, with former Brisbane Roar star Thomas Broich

– who yields to almost no one in his admiration for the man he still calls boss – admitting: 'You kind of crave a personal relationship with your coach but he was so authoritarian almost. You had so much respect for him, and you were almost scared to walk into his office, or ask for a favour.

'But he was a very good person. When I had personal problems, he allowed me to fly back to Germany midseason, like, we had games at the weekend, and he said: "Go back for three days, come back and the only thing I expect from you is to play well." In a way, he's a very good human being.

'But there was never a chance of small talk or anything like that. You do miss that as a player, and you don't want to be scared all the time. But in hindsight I understand the kind of atmosphere he created was of high expectations, of intensity and the pressure that was there on a daily basis was required for us to become such a successful football team.

'And there was a lot of reverse psychology going on. Like, when we played our best football, he was very, very critical. There was one game when he basically made fun of us, we were leading 4–0 at half-time and we played the best football we've ever played. We come into the dressing room, and everyone was so cheerful, proud, happy, and so motivated to get going and play football, we loved the day and loved our jobs, we loved each other basically, it felt like the best day ever. Then we sat down, he came in and everyone went very quiet. It was like: "Oh, shit, what's happening now?" And then he said something along the lines of: "Yeah, you might be four-nil up, but does anyone think this is any good?"

'And we were all like, shit, what is happening? This can't be true. And then he stopped for a bit, laughed, and said: "Just kidding, guys." It was spectacular. But we always believed it – because he was like that, he always found something that needed to be better and where we needed to improve.'

That's been a common theme throughout his career, naturally. Nobody reaches the top by deciding that a mid-table finish and mediocrity on the training field is even remotely acceptable. And, if it means sacrificing a few good meals and laugh-out-loud moments with the guys who share his ultimate goals and ambitions, that's clearly OK.

Way back in his early days at South Melbourne, when he was just cutting his teeth as a coach, Ange used to turn up at the board meeting every Tuesday night. Right after training, at about 8.30 p.m., he'd stroll in and make contributions to a meeting that would rumble on until maybe midnight, as the combination of old-school Greek directors and younger appointees discussed every aspect of running Australia's most successful club at a time when they had to fight for everything. Then, when things broke up, he'd join some of the newer directors at the McDonald's on the corner of Clarendon Street and City Road, taking part in what one of those involved called 'the unofficial board meeting' that would run until about 1 a.m., on a good night. Burgers with the boys, then? Surely not. Ah, but he had a reason for these semi-social excursions. Making sure the more forward-thinking elements of the board understood what he really needed, if South were to keep winning Grand Finals, have a crack at the Oceania Championship . . . and make it all the way to the inaugural FIFA World Club Championship Finals. Even over a Big Mac and coffee, with Ange, it was all business.

Key Game

SOUTH MELBOURNE 2 CARLTON SC 1

Olympic Park, Melbourne
16 May 1998

POSTECOGLOU'S first Grand Final as manager, seven years on from lifting the trophy as captain, is widely considered one of the most entertaining games in Aussie soccer history. There was certainly plenty to admire in a game between one of the country's traditional 'ethnic' footballing powerhouses and Aussie Rules royalty looking to muscle in on 'soccer'.

While fans of other clubs will argue over the fine details, Carlton are almost certainly the biggest and most historic AFL team in all of Australia. They also happen to count Ange among their most ardent supporters; if 'footy' will always be his second favourite sport, there's no doubt about his number one team in this uniquely combative mishmash of rugby, GAA and ultra-endurance running. There is no other code of football quite like it. And few brands carry as much resonance as the famous Blues.

When the two Melbourne clubs met for a Grand Final in their home city, then, it felt as if plenty was at stake. Not least for the Greek-Australian community – second and third generation though some of them might be – who still made up a large section of the South/Hellas support.

Beaten finalists in five of the six previous seasons, Postecoglou's men did not dominate possession or territory in the way he would have liked. But a Con Boutsianis winner 90 seconds from the end of regulation time was enough to see South edge a contest that had seen striker John Anastasiadis score an early opener against his brother, Dean, in goal for Carlton. Marcus Stergiopoulos equalised for the Blues with 12 minutes remaining. But Ange's boys found a way to win, sparking wild celebrations – pyros, partying and proper old-school European-style scenes of jubilation on the terracing – among supporters who had waited seven long years to see their team, who had finished top of the National Soccer League, crowned champions via Australia's play-off system.

Winning that first trophy as manager was obviously a major turning point in Postecoglou's career, giving him even greater confidence in what he was doing, his belief strengthened even further when South won the title again the following season. In the wider context of Australian football, however, it meant much more than merely a good start for a young coach.

South Melbourne president Nicholas Maikousis singled this game out when asked to name a favourite memory of one game from Ange's time at the helm, picking it ahead of even their glorious win at the Oceania Championship or facing Manchester United in the World Club Championship at Rio's famous Maracanã.

'That's very much a personal question,' said Maikousis. 'And it was probably the first Grand Final against Carlton. And Carlton is a historic AFL football club – footy club – here, right? You know them. Well, they ventured into the soccer space and created Carlton Soccer Club effectively. It lasted a very short period of time but flourished. For a very short period of time, they actually were strong, both on and off the park. They probably lasted a year or two, tops [Carlton folded early in their fourth season due to financial difficulties].

'But they made it into the Grand Final that first year. And my father passed away a couple of, I think, two days before the semi, from memory. So, it was all pretty raw for me. So, that was a very, very emotional time. But, you know, it was big for a lot of people, for a lot of reasons, right across the whole community. There were brothers playing against each other. They had come in as a new full-time professional outfit, not one of the old ethnic, old-school, part-timers still. They were a threat. And we won in a great game. It felt really important at the time.'

Chapter 11

JAPANESE BOY

IN HINDSIGHT, of course, it seems like a match made, sanctioned and blessed by the highest authorities in the sporting heavens; Ange Postecoglou's almost religious devotion to the principles of hard work, perseverance and the pursuit of forward momentum puts him pretty much in lockstep with the central tenets of Japanese culture. So, yeah, his time at Yokohama F. Marinos was always going to pan out beautifully for all involved, right? He just walked in, took charge of a squad eager to embrace new ideas – and immediately implemented a revolutionary style of football guaranteed to deliver J.League success. No dissent, no slip-ups, no notes? No chance.

The truth, according to those who shared a dressing room with the Aussie coach trying to make it big in Japan, is that Postecoglou overcame enormous internal opposition at Yokohama. Finding himself confronted by a squad united in their belief that the club had made a horrible mistake, branded an outsider with dangerously reckless ideas that could only end in disaster, he was far from guaranteed to achieve anything notable in an entirely alien environment.

Naoki Imaya, who acted as interpreter and go-between for Postecoglou and assistant Peter Cklamovski during that difficult first season at Yokohama, still chuckles at the memory of translating Ange's best intentions and biggest ideas for a group of players who gave off an unmistakable air of hostility, every word serving only to further antagonise professional footballers who refused to listen – to really listen – and learn. He recalls with great clarity, too, the bathhouse confrontation with experienced team leaders giving voice to their deepest misgivings about this new gaffer, clearly some sort of foolhardy maverick intent on undermining all the hard work they'd put into maintaining the team's top-flight status. Like Ange himself, Imaya can laugh about it now.

Because it's something of a recurring theme, this, isn't it? The winning over of doubters. The clearing out of confirmed non-believers, even if that means turning over 25 players in a single season. The absolute refusal to compromise on core beliefs. All ending in not merely triumph, but a lasting legacy far surpassing all expectations.

Yet there were a few extra kinks to the same old story that would play out in Japan. A language barrier to surmount. A culture shock to be absorbed. Navigating his way through new footballing territory, figuring out where he needed to modify the message and deciding upon which sacred ground he absolutely had to stand firm, made Postecoglou's working life all the more difficult. But the struggles also made Yokohama's coronation as champions in 2019 – courtesy of a final-day victory over their nearest rivals, no less – one of the sweetest moments in a managerial career not exactly short on high points.

In Japan, Postecoglou is now revered as someone who changed the country's football forever. Not just by proving that a more adventurous tactical approach could work in a competition that had always veered towards rigidity and discipline, but by changing attitudes and resetting the ambitions of a footballing nation unsure of its own place in the world.

Yet, by his own admission, he could hardly have picked a more difficult setting for his next step in football following his shock departure from the Socceroos in late 2017. Not only was he taking over a team threatened with relegation. But he would have to work wonders without recourse to his go-to solution for almost every problem.

'How was I going to be able to implement my ideas, when I've got a pretty clear sense of how I want a team to play, but the most powerful tool I use is language?' is how, in a 2019 interview with Australian media, he framed the question confronting him upon arrival in Japan, adding: 'And that's been taken away from me.'

He found the answer in a new emphasis on analysis through video, learning the value of showing as much as telling players. Focusing on this element had some very definite spin-off benefits as a coach, among them the advent of his favourite 'inverted full backs' tactic now so popular at all levels of the game.

He also went out of his way to appoint one particular member of staff. In Imaya, he found a former player – and aspiring coach – who would act as a conduit between the English-speaking backroom staff and a squad seemingly dead set against him from the outset. In time, the pair would effectively speak with one voice, allowing Postecoglou to tap into the emotions of players. So in sync were they that the head coach could dive headlong into deep themes of childhood and family, delivering speeches that his old colleague describes as utterly inspirational.

Imaya, who had met Postecoglou about a year before his appointment at Yokohama, when the Socceroos had visited Japan for a pre-World Cup friendly, left a coaching job at a lower-league club in order to act as interpreter for the new arrival, revealing: 'I'd been at that club for eight years. So there was obviously some feeling towards that club and it was tough to leave. But, at the same time, what an opportunity to be right next to Ange. With me wanting to become a manager in the future, I thought: "Wow, some people would pay just to work alongside Ange for one year."'

Once he'd completed possibly the most straightforward contract negotiations in footballing history, Imaya went to work. And found himself caught in the middle of a situation that, at times, seemed utterly irreconcilable. A setting where every word had to be measured with great care.

You know the old joke, right? The one about how many interpreters it takes to change a light bulb? Well, obviously it depends on the context . . . That rather sums up the multilingual juggling act performed by Imaya every time he stepped into the dressing room to translate a team talk. The fact that he could see the mistrust and feel the malevolence of this captive audience didn't exactly help. And, on the off chance that he wasn't picking up on the very strong vibes whenever the boss set foot inside the dressing room, he was quickly given a very clear message about the depth of animosity towards the new man.

Imaya, whose family moved to Australia when he was ten before he returned to Japan to follow his football ambitions, fell back on the linguistic flourishes of his adopted homeland as he recalled: 'Aw, mate, we went into camp in the first few days. We went to Okinawa, I think, for a training camp just after Ange and Pete arrived. I remember going into the bathhouse and hot spring area. And oh, the players were on me straight away: "Come on, this guy doesn't know what he's talking about . . . we've hired the wrong guy . . . I've never heard so many complaints in ten years at Yokohama F. Marinos . . ."

'I could have just said yeah, and gone along with the players. But I felt I had to stand up and say: "Look, he's a top manager. Trust in him." From then on, the players didn't come back to me with any of their complaints, because they clearly realised I wasn't going to listen, that I believed in what Ange was doing.

'Obviously I do remember how uncertain or even opposed to Ange certain players were. I remember it clearly because, when he was giving his speeches, I was standing right next to him, sensing the vibrations coming from the group; I could feel the energy of players sitting there and clearly thinking: "Mmm, this isn't going to work . . ."

'If I learned one thing from Ange, it's that people can crumble or lose their words in those situations. They start stuttering. But Ange had this pure belief in his words. That helped him so much at the start. Because if he's not sure and I'm not sure, and I feel the negative energy coming back from players who aren't going with him, I can't feel that same energy from the boss. That would have made it very hard for me to get the message across.

'But by that stage in his career he was so determined, so intent. He had this belief in how we had to play football.

The only way to play football. If we were going to be successful, that was the only way it was going to be possible.

'He was very bold, in a way. Yokohama F. Marinos had
been a counter-attacking team, very defensive. But from
the pre-season camp under Ange and Peter, we were very
aggressive offensively and defensively. With the ball, we
were very attack-minded. And it was about players moving
everywhere, rotations and automatic movement.

'The biggest difference was how quick things were. This
wasn't the tempo Japanese players were used to. At times,
they felt they needed to just relax and keep the ball a little
bit. Ange wasn't having that.

'We weren't getting the right results at the start, so obviously players were thinking: "Ah, okay, this isn't working.
The coach doesn't know what he's talking about. He doesn't
understand Japanese football. It doesn't work here. We've
got to slow it down a bit." They didn't always say so much
in words, but you could see they had this doubt over the
way he wanted to play, attacking wise and defensively.'

Tactically, everything was built around a 4-3-3. So far, so
familiar. But the first incarnation of Ange-ball at Yokohama
wasn't quite the same as the model he took to Glasgow and
then London, Imaya recalling: 'Going back to that first
camp, he actually had the full backs out wide. They would
be in the widest lanes, providing width. But he brought
them inside – the inverted full backs – a couple of weeks
later. I remember we were reviewing a training match and
he noticed that the passing distance of Japanese players
wasn't as strong, in a way, as Westerners. He wanted the
distances to be shorter, so he tucked the full backs inside.
But yeah, in general it was a 4-3-3. He started playing with

one No. 6, a single defensive midfielder. And, when they won the title in 2019, they went with a double pivot, two defensive midfielders.

'It was all radically different from what other teams were doing in 2018. Back then, there were maybe one or two teams who tried to play as drastically and openly as Ange. Even they didn't come close to what he wanted to do.'

Initial opposition to the Postecoglou method wasn't restricted to footballers who simply didn't fancy a change of pace, with Imaya remembering how 'senior people' at the club had voiced their concerns in that first season; the fact that they felt emboldened enough to complain to him, already established as one of the head coach's closest confidants, tells you how difficult that first year was.

Imaya, who uses the word 'tense' to describe a campaign where the club only just avoided relegation, remembers Postecoglou accepting that criticism was inevitable. Until he could turn the club around, he'd just have to put up with the sniping from the sidelines. Even the odd grenade being lobbed from the directors' box.

'But look at the J.League now,' he said. 'They all want to play how Ange played. It's a direct legacy from what he did. To my mind, he changed the course of Japanese football. Not just tactically but mentally, as well. He played unbelievable football, really exciting football that people now want to play. They realised that we could actually get results and win the league by doing that. But he was really the first to do it. And that took a lot of leadership.

'His admiration of Japanese players goes back to even before he came here. He always had a respect and fondness for them, for how they played and what they could do.

When he was coaching the Socceroos against Japan, in fact, I always got the impression that he would rather have been working with the Japanese players! He loved the way they played the game. And that's another reason why he wanted to come and work in the J.League.

'It was like he couldn't understand why Japanese coaches would want to play such boring football, if I can call it that; certainly less entertaining football. He knew there were quality players in Japan. So he was thinking: "Why didn't you play attacking football? You've got the right players to do it. I know they can do it." He proved it. That's how it started.'

Wherever there is a revolution of thought, of course, there are inevitable casualties. In football, players who either can't or won't buy into a new style of play never last long. Some may be more difficult to move on, with status, length of contract, declining market value and other factors often getting in the way of a coach's desire for a clean sweep. The fact that Yokohama were owned by the City Football Group almost certainly made life easier for Postecoglou, though. Quietly waiting for success isn't in the DNA of an organisation whose bankrolling of Manchester City is indicative of an impatient desire to win everything, everywhere, all at once.

Former assistant Cklamovski, who stayed behind in Japan to become a manager in his own right when Postecoglou jumped to the Scottish Premiership, explained: 'Oh, 2018 was a roller coaster. We got the football going rapidly and, although there were doubts, it was a quick uptake in how we were playing. CFG, the City Football Group, at the time were amazed at how quickly we generated this football, but throughout the year, the results were a little bit like a roller coaster. A few reasons for that but the football, and even the metrics behind that, was there. There was success coming.

'It was hard to stop, and if you look at the first 12 months of our time at Marinos, we turned over around 25, maybe even 30 players. And 2019, of course, was the trophy year – but 2018 was scarily close to relegation. There were periods that were uncertain, let's say. But, to their credit, the owners and CFG believed in Ange, supported him in some windows and ultimately got their rewards.

'That's what's important with Ange: building an identity at a club. Obviously, Ange's legacy is at the club, and it continues on now. It surpasses time, even longer than he stays, and that's everything for him. The football club want that football every weekend and that's the legacy of Ange at Yokohama F. Marinos. No doubt, that's what he intended to do at Celtic for as long as he was there and then beyond his time, for it to grow and continue to evolve. And that's really important for him. He's a pure football man and that's everything to him.

'I also know he loved his time here. First and foremost, Japan is such a beautiful country, and that connects to the football culture here. In Japan, football and baseball are the big sports. But they love football there. And the level of football should be recognised, it's a higher level of football than people think. It's tough and it's competitive. It really hones your skills as a coach or manager, because there are so many good teams here and it's so competitive – so it makes sure you're razor-sharp in your game preparation. That just refines our work. Yokohama F. Marinos is a fantastic story to tell because we started in 2018, after qualifying for the World Cup, and Ange makes the decision to come here and, luckily enough, I came along as part of that journey.'

If Postecoglou had an influence on Japanese football, it's obvious that the game there left its mark on him as a coach. Not just because much of his Celtic success can be traced back to the recruitment of players like Kyogo Furuhashi, Reo Hatate and Daizen Maeda. The lessons he learned in the J.League, the skills he acquired in terms of honing his messaging, are evident in how he works to this day. The experience improved him as a coach. And it proved that the foundations around which he builds a team are adaptable to different grounds and new conditions. If it works in both Brisbane and Yokohama, it'll work in Glasgow. Or London . . .

Asked about the cultural challenges that face any newcomers to Japanese society, Imaya was quick to point out how well Postecoglou and Cklamovski took to the new situation. Unsurprisingly, Ange admired the famous sense of reserve that so many outsiders mistake for a lack of passion; he wasn't fooled for a minute.

'Nothing changes in terms of them being good managers, good coaches and good people, just because they've moved country,' said Imaya. 'But there are certain things that you have to maybe take in, because there is a cultural difference. There are going to be things that are different, if I can generalise it, for Westerners than they are for Asians. But, at the end of the day, you're still dealing with people. Over a period of time, players realised that Ange was original and authentic. If you can manage that, the message will get across. If Ange had gone away from his authenticity, tried to change his approach just because he was dealing with Japanese people, it wouldn't have worked.

'He could have gone in and listened to everyone who said: "You can't do this or that in Japan. That's not how things are done there." But Ange and Peter would have lost their touch, lost the thing that makes them good coaches. So being authentic was important. And I felt that from the first couple of days.

'It wasn't arrogance. They didn't come in and say: "This is my way or the highway, you do it or you're out." It wasn't that. But he was himself.

'It definitely helped that I had been a player, that I had coached. Because you can interpret or translate his message word for word. But we're dealing with people, so you need to get the right message across. Sometimes you have to read between the lines, think to yourself: "Right, what is he trying to say here? What does he want to say? Because if I just translate that word for word, the real message won't get to the players." It helps, knowing what it feels like to be in that position. Being an ex-player myself, I know that the choice of words by a manager hits you – in a good way but also in a bad way, I guess.

'There was no specific game or day when things changed for them. I do remember, though, that our fourth game of the season was away to Urawa Reds. They're still a big team but back then they were really strong. We'd had a draw and two losses going into that game. Being a manager, 95 per cent of them might say the right things: "We're going to attack, we're going for a win here . . . blah, blah, blah." But, as a player, you'd feel that the manager will be happy for a point, to get away with a draw or maybe a scrappy win.

'Ange refused to do that. You could tell that he was absolutely determined on how we should play the game, that he couldn't accept playing any other way. He would not take a step backwards. And it's so easy, as a manager, to sway that way, just a little bit. But Ange wasn't just saying the words. The players felt that, yeah, this is the way we have to play.

'During that first year, when we started winning league games and got to the League Cup final [losing 1–0 to Shonan Bellmare], there was a change. By halfway through the season, you still couldn't say that everyone believed. But one became two, two became six or seven players . . . they started showing a real passion for the way we played. Now they wanted to prove, to everyone in Japanese football, that this could be done. And that was the message from Ange. It struck a chord with the players.

'He was always on it, too. Even when we won games. I remember we beat Kashima 3–0 at home, but Ange didn't think we played well. And he absolutely slaughtered the players in the changing room. It's a recurring theme, isn't it? Okay, glad to know it wasn't just us! It was actually so good to see that, as someone who was trying to assist him. It reminded me that he is always true to his word because, okay, we won the game 3–0. But we didn't play the way we should have. He knew that we needed to keep playing our way if we were ever going to achieve consistent success.

'What did he want from us? To be number one. You have to be trying to be number one in your position, your role within the club and team. You have to be trying to get better every day. If you're on the medical staff, a translator, a coach, if you're satisfied and okay with what you've done now, and aren't trying to get better for tomorrow and next week . . . I think you won't last. I just think that's an absolute must, a non-negotiable. You won't work for him long if you don't have that drive.'

The same rules applied to the man himself. He refused to accept good enough when it came to his own efforts. He never even thought of cutting himself some slack during his time in Japan; there was no chance of him hiding behind the language barrier and just accepting that he couldn't possibly have the same hold over players as he did back home in Melbourne, where there was no chance of being misunderstood. So much of management, after all, is about the psychology of what is said. Or left unsaid. You can't climb on to even the lowest rungs of the professional coaching ladder without listening to experts talk about team building and the importance of personal relationships, or sitting through lectures with themes like 'Just because you taught it, doesn't mean they learned it', subtitled: 'Everyone sees the world through the lens of their own experience.' The message matters. Every word of it. Surely there was some drop-off in the famous Postecoglou rhetorical powers when everything had to go through the filter of a third party?

Imaya is adamant that nothing was lost in translation, insisting: 'His speeches were emotional. Hugely emotional. And inspiring. Okay, some coaches' speeches tend to be repetitive sometimes. They have to be if you're going to get the message across. So there would be themes. But he had a good way of keeping their attention, emphasising how great it was to play this game.

'He would always talk to players about what it was like when they were kids, five years old and starting to play football: "Did you give the ball away to your brother or did you want to keep it? When you went to the park, I'm sure you had the soccer ball at your feet and wanted to keep the ball. We need to keep the ball. If the ball isn't right there under your feet, go and grab it from the opposition. Go back to your childhood . . ." Speeches like that would make players emotional. And he always had stories to tell.

'He would always say that nobody came to the game of football by themselves. There were always coaches, parents, people who helped them through the game. So, whenever a player was making their debut for the club, he would say: "Remember the names of everyone who helped you get here. You play for them today." It was inspiring.'

Postecoglou went to Japan seeking adventure. He left after four years because he yearned for an opportunity in Europe; the decision to look for openings on the other side of the world was conveyed to his agent well in advance of Celtic's approach. There's no doubt that a number of big clubs passed on him. Decided that someone who had 'only' done it in Japan – don't even talk about Brisbane or Melbourne – wasn't worth the risk.

If his achievements at Celtic and subsequent recruitment by Spurs forced some of those chairmen and chief executives to regret not looking more closely at a candidate who clearly is, to quote one City Football Group executive, 'the real deal', the success of one man should also force a rethink on the value of the experiences he went through in Japan. A footballing country that was no mere extended stopover on Ange's journey from Australia to Europe. But a vital part of his development.

Key Game

YOKOHAMA F. MARINOS 3 TOKYO FC 0

7 December 2019

WITH this victory, Ange Postecoglou secured one of the biggest honours – at the time – ever claimed by an Australian coach. And proved a point. In a dressing room where he had translators speaking three different languages – Japanese, obviously, but also Portuguese and Thai – at the same time, his belief in keeping team talks short, sharp and to the point was tested to the full. But he made it work. Introduced the idea of inverted full backs. And went all out for victory, even in the final game, when Yokohama merely needed to avoid a four-goal defeat in order to clinch the J.League title. Yeah, because he was going to sit in and play for a nil-nil . . .

Nobody involved in Ange's transition to Japanese culture and football pretends that everything went smoothly. Marinos didn't avoid relegation by all that comfortable a margin in his first season, although they did reach the J.League Cup final. On a personal level, the passing of dad Jim carried obvious significance for someone who insists his entire career was built on a desire to please his father.

Asked after his J.League triumph what his father might have said to him, in the wake of a victory that had many hailing him as the greatest football coach in Australian history, Postecoglou grinned and said: 'He probably would have said I got my tactics wrong at the start, because we started a bit slowly. And then he would have praised me.'

Chapter 12

A CELTIC LOVE AFFAIR, EVENTUALLY

THAT old adage about a picture being worth a thousand words? As someone effectively paid by the line, there's a natural reluctance to go along with anything that diminishes the value of a carefully crafted paragraph or ten. But a handful of prints handed over in the restaurant of a suburban Melbourne hotel bar – the sort of place that has banks of busily beeping and clattering 'pokies' (Vegas-style slot machines) in one corner and a group of cheerfully unsteady punters taking part in some crazy sweep on horse races in the other – couldn't fail to force a re-evaluation. Only a 24-carat idiot fails to recognise solid gold when it's staring them in the face.

The photographs former South Melbourne and Socceroos defender Steve Blair so kindly allowed us to use for this book are, quite simply, nothing short of sensational. Ange Postecoglou posing outside the front door of Celtic Park. Decades before he was ushered in, to no great initial acclaim, as manager. Ange jokingly squeezing into a turnstile at the ground he now calls his match-day home, with his goatee beard and mischievous grin making him look very much like a young Billy Connolly. Joining close pal and team-mate Blair to hold a replica of the European Cup. Or paying respects at the shrine to Brother Walfrid. All remarkable. Like the story behind the holiday snaps, which capture the excitement of a young Greek-Australian with a passion for football, in general. But no specific fascination with the team he would later lead from the technical area. If it took a while for Celtic fans to wholeheartedly embrace a manager too quickly dismissed as an unknown no-hoper by some who should have known better, it's also true to say that the famous Hoops did not provoke a love-at-first-sight response from Postecoglou. No matter how persistently Drumchapel boy Blair – eagerly claiming a seat next to his best buddy on those long interstate flights that made the old National Soccer League such a test of endurance – pressed the claim of the team he adored.

Postecoglou's ability to read the room meant he was never going to pitch up, on the day of his appointment as Celtic's 19th manager back in the summer of 2021, and deliver some Brendan Rodgers-style snow job spiel about his life-long love of the boys in green. Former Liverpool boss Rodgers, who shamelessly hammed up his status as a Celtic supporter raised on tales of glories past, rather infamously couldn't get away quickly enough when a better opportunity came along in February 2019, the Northern Irishman dashing down the road to Leicester City less than three years into his 'dream job' – now his again, of course – in Glasgow. Nor could Ange ever compare himself to any of the more bona fide 'Celtic men' to have preceded him in the role of manager; he was never going to sell himself as a diehard like Neil Lennon, whom he succeeded, or a beloved figure like the late Tommy Burns, who always said that the biggest problem with managing 'his' team was being too close and caring too greatly.

As dedicated as he would be to the job, as passionate as he would become about the supporters' belief that Celtic are every bit as deserving of the '*més que un club*' status so readily claimed by Barcelona, he wasn't daft enough to concoct a connection that wouldn't stand up to close inspection. His first footballing loves? South Melbourne Hellas, of course. And the mighty Liverpool side – Kenny Dalglish remains his hero, to this day – who dominated European football in the 1970s and 1980s.

Blair actually latched on to Dalglish's early career at Celtic as a hook he might use to convert Postecoglou. The former centre half is entitled to think that, in some strange way, his relentless propaganda campaign on behalf of his home-town team had some effect. Eventually. Yet he couldn't have believed, when he was accompanying a much younger Ange around not merely Celtic Park but also Ibrox, that he was in the presence of a future Parkhead boss.

Blair, who has retained a good 90 per cent of his Glaswegian accent despite his family emigrating to Victoria when he was just 12, laughed as he handed over the photos and explained: 'I used to go back to Glasgow all the time, every close season. We'd play, the season would finish, then I'd go.

'One of the times I went, I think he was going to London, so I said he should come up. He came up and stayed with me. We went to football grounds and organised a tour of Celtic Park – and Ibrox, as well. He did all those tours. I didn't actually take him to a physical game but I took him on a tour of Celtic Park and Ibrox. He'd been in Drumchapel, where I was from, so he knew all about it.

'That's why his story is amazing. Can you imagine someone picking up your book about this coach, Ange Postecoglou, and you look at where he came from and all the difficulties he's been through.

'I'd have never imagined he'd be Celtic manager – not that he wouldn't be good enough, but what he needed was the opportunity. It's just a crazy story.

'That first visit to Celtic Park, we would've been in our twenties. Look at the picture of him squeezing into one of the really narrow old-fashioned turnstiles ... who would have predicted what would happen 25 or 30 years later? He was such a lover of the game. Crowds, players, they all excited him. But we might not always agree. I was always trying to drill into him my love of Celtic, which just seems crazy now, you know? I was always trying to drill it into his head. Nah, nah, nah, he wasn't having it! But I guess, if you throw enough mud, some of it sticks. I'd say Celtic this, Celtic that – but he was fixed on Liverpool.'

Often found with his head in a book about Bill Shankly or studying the latest developments at Anfield, Postecoglou the player wasn't particularly in the market for another European team to support back when he was captaining South Melbourne to title triumphs – and trying to emulate some of the high standards set in the red half of Merseyside. That didn't stop Blair from trying.

'He loved Dalglish, as well,' said the former defender, an inductee into both the South Melbourne FC and Socceroos Halls of Fame. 'So, when he looked at Kenny's history, saw he'd started out at Celtic, that got him interested. Then finding out that both sets of supporters share "You'll Never Walk Alone" as a sort of terracing anthem. Isn't it just amazing how this has all worked out? He could've gone to any club, like Kilmarnock, or any Scottish club, he could've gone to Hearts or something. But he goes to the club that's got the "You'll Never Walk Alone" connection, the connection with Dalglish. Is it fate? Or just luck? Maybe it's fate and this was meant to happen.'

Whatever your views on kismet and destiny, it's generally accepted that nobody simply strolls into their dream job. What's the old Russian proverb? 'Pray. But keep rowing for shore.' Postecoglou never stopped pulling in the general direction of Europe, still the first-choice destination of anyone involved in Australian football. But he suffered a lot of knock-backs before Celtic agreed to take a chance on a gaffer who, lest we forget, was pretty much every supporter's second choice – at best – when he stepped into a berth apparently reserved for Eddie Howe. Persistence is a narrative pillar of the Postecoglou story. He needed it, given the general level of ignorance and insularity that confronted his every attempt – one brief and predictably chaotic spell in the Greek lower leagues aside – to make it on the continent where football was first invented, codified and transformed into a business with enormous economic, social and cultural importance.

'I laugh when people talk about whether Ange is driven,' said Blair. 'He was getting doors closed on him all the time. He wanted to get out of Australia – but all the doors in Europe were shut. They would all say the same thing: "Who are you? Postecoglou? What have you done? Oh, Australia. Nah, we'll give it a miss. Socceroos coach? Australia? Nah." All those closed doors.

'In his early days, I mean, obviously, I thought he was a good coach – but he did have some hiccups. Ange's story is not all success. People just think he's done fantastic. He hasn't. He's had some rough experiences and some rough times, but he persisted with it, and he was dogged in the way he thought about playing the game.

'He was very successful with the Socceroos and then in Japan, so he started building some success. He just needed someone to say: "Here's an opening, here's a chance . . ." and that was it.'

Well, not quite. Scottish football can be a tiny bit insular, to say the least. And Celtic fans, in mutinous mood after seeing Lennon's attempt to land a record-breaking tenth consecutive league title collapse in disarray, weren't instantly won over by a left-field appointment too easily decried as a nobody by the less well-informed pundits and punters. Especially after being told, virtually all summer, that Howe was merely finalising a few minor details before sweeping into town with big plans and a proven pedigree in English football.

Blair admitted: 'See when he got the job? I'm telling you what! The amount of phone calls and texts I got from mates back home saying: "What the fuck? Who's this guy? What's going on? Is he for real?" Even I had my doubts. Not in his ability, because I knew he'd make something work. My doubt was whether they would persevere with him or give him enough time to implement what he wanted to implement. That was my fear.'

It says a great deal about Postecoglou that one of his first calls, on arrival in the manager's office at Celtic's training ground, was to the old pal who had spent so long bending his ear about his team, their history and the glorious future just waiting to be tapped by the right manager at the perfect time.

Revealing how confusion turned to delight when he answered a call from an unknown number, Blair said: 'I'm thinking: "Who the hell is this?" And he goes: "Hi Stevie, it's Ange. Guess where I am." That's what he says: "Guess where I am!"

' "I've got no idea, where are you?"

' "I'm sitting in the office at Lennoxtown."

' "Lennoxtown? What are you doing there?"

' "I've got the Celtic job!"

'I was so happy, I was bursting with pride. I was so happy for him. A couple of things from that. One, he took the time to ring me especially because he knew that'd have an impact on me, like, he knew what I'd be like with that. And two, I was just so stoked for him, that someone had finally opened up and given him that opportunity.'

It's pretty clear by now, of course, that Postecoglou and Celtic were that rare thing in football, a meeting of minds and alignment of visions. Ange talks with confidence about 'getting' the whole Celtic story. And, of course, his football – adventurous in the extreme, on occasion – fitted in perfectly with the club's sporting DNA. Even if not every single supporter enjoyed each bold stroke pulled by the gaffer.

More than one interviewee who contributed to this book could quote, almost word for word, some of the terminology used by Postecoglou at his very first press conference as Celtic manager. If some stumbled over a precise turn of phrase, all instantly recall his promise to do things a certain way.

Blair said: 'His first ever interview, he says: "I'm going to bring you an attacking style of football you will be proud of. You won't sit on your arse – you're going to stand up and applaud it." Well, what happened? Absolutely what he promised. When you talk to Celtic supporters, they say they hadn't seen Celtic play like that for years.

'The way they invited the opposition to press them, it shows you how much the game's moved on. It's a different game. To have the balls to do that, I applaud that. I don't agree with a lot of it – I'm more your old standard centre half who wants to get it up the pitch!

'But I applaud it. I've come to understand how the game all fits together. He believes that, if we've got the ball and they're running about, when they tire that's when holes open up and that's when we make our mark.

'Even me, when I was watching Celtic in Europe, I'm thinking: "Just sit back!" In one of the games when we were one or two up, I'm shouting at the telly: "Just hold it now!" But he's had that philosophy a long time. And the good thing about Ange is that it's based on a lot of knowledge. From a very early age, he was just crazy about learning everything he could. He had this thirst for football. He'd read everything about it, he'd watch DVDs – well, it was video tapes at the time – about it. Games, club histories, all sorts of stuff like that. A bit of analysis and stats, so he was just so passionate about it.

'Now, there's a million kids who are passionate about it. What's the difference with him? The difference was that he did something with that passion. He tried things, tried to implement things, and not all of it was successful. But it's paying off now.'

There's also a natural connection and like-mindedness, many feel, between the culture at South Melbourne and the

Celtic story. Both clubs founded by immigrants, both fiercely proud of their Greek and Irish roots, respectively, and they are sporting institutions created out of necessity – and allowed to grow organically.

'He's got an affinity with the reason Celtic were formed,' said Blair, a proud member of South's Team of the Century whose status as a third-generation Hoops fan makes him ideally placed to compare the two. 'It's about community. And South Melbourne was all about community as well. He talks about the tradition of support being passed down, like me from my dad, my grandad and so it goes. He understands all that.

'For example, Ange's dad was so proud of him playing for South Melbourne, absolutely. And it's the same with Celtic supporters – they are proud of that team. Absolutely we are. It's not just a football club, it means more. That's the thing he understands. Some other manager might walk in and think: "It's just a football club." It's not just a football club. And he understands it's not just a football club. It means more to people than just football, doesn't it?'

Postecoglou appeared to have struck exactly the right tone as an 'outsider' buying into the best traditions of Celtic, on and off the park. Although football remained his priority, he showed himself to be in possession of a social conscience, speaking up in praise of those who are working to help refugees settle in Australia – and drawing direct comparisons between two clubs thousands of miles apart.

Speaking to Australian sports channel Stan Sport in February 2022, he said of Celtic: 'Their whole background and why the actual club was formed, to feed poor Irish immigrants, there was a purpose behind this club that stayed with it right to this day.

'For me that resonates obviously strongly, being an immigrant in our own country. And South Melbourne Hellas, Melbourne Croatia, Sydney Croatia, all these clubs were set up the same way. They weren't set up solely to be football clubs, they were set up to help people adjust to life in their new land.'

Postecoglou is quietly proud to have found such a meaningful role in football. Whatever the restrictions, inconveniences and heart-tearing frustrations of the job may have been, the Celtic managerial gig remained a much-coveted position. Ange enjoyed the status that came with it. Appreciated being able to invite friends into the inner sanctum at a club known all over the world.

Former South Melbourne team-mate Tim Schleiger, one of those to have flown in specially to see Ange in his new environment, brings a typically uproarious Aussie sensibility to his travel diary from the trip, revelling in the perks that go along with being able to drop one particular name into every conversation.

Schleiger, forced out of the game through injury at 22, and now a respected sports science expert who has worked with athletes from youth footballers to current Olympians, revealed: 'It's really funny because, when you arrived at the airport in Glasgow, the first thing people would say is: "Aww, mate, the accent!" Of course, I just happened to say: "Yeah, a mate of mine coaches one of the teams here . . ." And then it's like: "Wait. You know Ange?" I don't reckon I paid a taxi driver, I don't think we fucking paid for a beer while we were there!

'For me, his success at Celtic didn't surprise me in any sense. I look at Ange and there is not a stone unturned, there is not a book that he hasn't read on man management, there is not a course, not one thing that he has left unturned. So, if he comes across as self-assured or stubborn or arrogant, I just look at it and go: "No, that does not surprise me." And it's well deserved because he's fucking worked for all of it.

'That's why he can make comments like, you know, those initial press conferences where he said: "You'll remember what I've said now by the end of the season." It doesn't surprise me. He's confident enough to do what needs to be done.'

It certainly took confidence for Postecoglou to take on the Celtic job as a one-man managerial team, famously arriving without any back-up in the form of a trusted old pal or hand-picked assistant. Think about that for a minute. He walked into the coaches' room at Lennoxtown knowing only that John Kennedy and Gavin Strachan had been key players in Lennon's backroom staff, before taking interim control of the team over the closing months of the previous campaign. Hardly a badge of honour, given the season they'd just endured.

Howe, of course, claimed that he refused the Celtic job because the club wouldn't provide contracts for not one but *three* trusted lieutenants – Jason Tindall, Stephen Purches and Simon Weatherstone. Ange went a different way. Put himself in an environment where he knew nobody, without knowing whose nose might have been put out of joint by his arrival. Unsure of whom he could trust. Yet he sold them on his vision for the team. Convinced that his way wasn't just the right way, but the only way.

'It's an unbelievable story,' said Schleiger, who is still in regular contact with his old friend. 'I don't think people outside of the game realised that he'd gone into a new group. Obviously, the gaffer [Neil Lennon] fucked off but the other two assistants stayed. And I can tell you exactly what Ange would have said: "If you're not going to back me here, you're not going to be on board my train. This is the way we're playing football, whether you fucking like it or not. We're playing this way. You can have your opinions, but if you're not on board, fuck off." Maybe not those exact words, because he's more polite than me . . . but that would be the message.'

A year into his time as boss, Postecoglou decided to make one key change to his staff, drafting in Australian legend Harry Kewell to fill the gap left by Stephen McManus taking charge of Celtic B in the Lowland League. From the outside looking in, at least to those who hadn't paid particularly close attention, it looked like Ange reaching for the comfort of a familiar face, an old mate, to perform key duties as first team coach. That wasn't quite right, though, was it? There are reasons why former Crawley, Notts County, Oldham and Barnet boss Kewell – who was actually on his way to interview for a managerial job – was surprised to get the call from Glasgow.

'He brought in Harry but even the background story between Harry and Ange is funny enough,' said Schleiger. 'Ange basically ended Harry's international career by not taking him to the 2014 World Cup, so there wasn't great blood between those two. And it was only through Vinnie Grella [former Socceroo-turned-agent], who basically said: "Give Harry a chance. Because he does know the game."

And, again, the quality of Ange, he's like: "Yep, all right. Let's give him a go. Give him a chance. Let's get some Aussies involved."

'And when I spoke to them last, I heard that it was working really well. Harry has such self-belief that, particularly in that front four, because he can work with someone like a Jota and just go: "Mate, try it. It doesn't matter. It's a front four, try that shit. I want you to try that again."

'That is something that Ange wouldn't be able to offer but again it's the strength of the character of the man going: "Well, all right, Harry might have had not a great feeling towards me initially because of our past with me saying: 'Look, I'm not going to pick you for the World Cup. You're done.'" But there they were, winning trophies together.'

The football community in Australia is incredibly tight-knit and fiercely proud of anyone making a name for themselves on a bigger stage. The excitement generated by the playing success of superstar players like Kewell, in his days with Leeds and Liverpool, was mirrored by a buzz around Ange-ball and its incarnation at Celtic. Based on the number of people in Melbourne alone who informed me that they never missed a Celtic game, whatever the time difference, the Australian ratings for their matches must have been enormous for those two seasons.

Nick Dimitrakis, the Nunawading City head of football operations who still stays in touch with Postecoglou, said: 'Yeah, every game, every game. But we saw that here with Brisbane. We saw it when he went to Japan. We follow him and whatever team he's at. So we've seen it unfold. It's not new to us. It was new to probably the Scottish people . . .'

Celtic supporters at home and abroad will admit, if they're being honest, that it took some time for Postecoglou to achieve the cult status he was afforded by dint of that first Premiership title. Almost every footballing success story includes a run of poor results that leaves the hero on the ropes, looking as if one more solid blow to the solar plexus will leave them down and out. That was precisely the scenario facing Ange as he took his struggling and patched-up team to Pittodrie on a grey Sunday in early October 2021, with no shortage of punters and pundits predicting a knockout in round eight of the Scottish Premiership.

Celtic had been knocked out of the Champions League in the second qualifying round by Danish side FC Midtjylland. Pitched into the Europa League, they'd lost to AZ Alkmaar (2–1 away), Real Betis (4–3 away) and, most damagingly, Bayer Leverkusen (4–0 at Celtic Park) to sour the mood of supporters who also had domestic reasons for discontent. After seven rounds of league action, Celtic were sitting sixth. Sixth. A full six points off the pace set by Rangers. They'd been beaten by their nearest and dearest rivals at Ibrox, never a good thing for any Hoops boss, while Hearts and Livingston had also inflicted defeats on a team clearly struggling to adapt to Postecoglou's master plan.

In the week leading up to the Aberdeen game, Celtic had been held to a 1–1 draw at home by Dundee United, then suffered that absolute shellacking by Leverkusen. They travelled north to the Granite City having won just two of their previous eight games, in all competitions. And, with all due respect, not many were putting much stock in a 3–0 home victory over Ross County in the league – or Championship side Raith Rovers being defeated by the same scoreline in a League Cup stroll at Celtic Park.

With six minutes to go, a Dons team including former Celtic skipper Scott Brown were holding the visitors to a draw, Lewis Ferguson having cancelled out Kyogo Furuhashi's 11th-minute opener with a header from a set piece early in the second half. Knives were being sharpened. Disgruntlement was very much in the air. And then substitute Tom Rogic created that half-yard of space that has become his trademark, playing in young overlapping left back Adam Montgomery, who crossed for Jota to finish from close range. A turning point? Ange certainly thought so.

Looking back on events about a year into his tenure, he insisted that he expected a rough start to his first season with a team in transition, pointing out that he'd been forced to throw players into games long before they were ready; Kyogo featured as a late sub in the league opener against Hearts at Tynecastle despite only meeting his new teammates at the pre-match meal, while Carl Starfelt started that game without having taken part in a single training session with Celtic.

Speaking to the Currie Club podcast, Postecoglou admitted that he'd been trying to speed up the team-building process, confessed that the initial results had been 'chaotic', yet insisted: 'I thought if I could get through that initial period quickly, I had a real belief that when the team was up and running, the football we play would have an impact. Wherever I've worked, that's been the cornerstone of what I've done.'

Nobody disputes the idea that the win at Pittodrie carried enormous significance. It's interesting, though, that the

manager didn't focus on how it might have changed percep-
tions of his team among a supporter base growing under-
standably nervous as they watched Rangers disappear over
the horizon – but on the effect it had on the internal chem-
istry of his squad, declaring: 'I thought it [Pittodrie] was a
bigger moment for the players than the fans. I sensed before
that the fans could see something was happening. We'd had
a couple of big wins before that at home. We'd had two
6–0s [against Dundee and St Mirren] and Kyogo had scored
a hat-trick, so they could see some seeds there. But that
game was really important for the players. Winning away
from home gains so much belief, especially at Aberdeen
which is a tough place to go.

'The way we won, scoring late. That's when I felt the
pendulum shifted for the players. Up until then I had kind
of been saying to them: "Bide your time and it will kick in."
And I think that after that game the players felt: "Okay, this
is the moment he's been talking about." '

For those invested in seeing Postecoglou thrive in a
hostile environment, the significance of Celtic managing to
snatch a late victory against Aberdeen certainly wasn't
underestimated, with plenty back in Oz staying up into the
wee small hours to witness that key moment in the Ange-
ball evolution. For someone like Dimitrakis, tuning in was
partly a matter of devotion. But also because concern over
how things were going would have made sleep difficult, at
best.

'We loved watching that Celtic team,' he said with a
laugh, adding: 'We talk about non negotiables, right? It was
Aberdeen in that first season and, I think, five minutes to
go. And the draw was not going to be good, it was not good

enough. And you can hear the commentator at the end, he's going: "This is not good enough. You're just going left to right, left to right. The draws are not gonna be good enough."

'Basically, Ange, he's waited for that. The plan has been to work the opposition side to side, then hit them in the gap that opens up. And we've seen it happen a lot of times. A lot of times. In Grand Finals with Brisbane, in a lot of games. And that moment came in the 90th minute or whatever.

'So Celtic get the win. And everything changes for Ange from that day. From that day. Five minutes left, your job is pretty much on the line at one-all, and your non-negotiables are still going. There were no long balls into the box for a second ball. He didn't do any of that. As the game started, it finished the same way. And then everything changed from that game. You go back and watch it, it's fascinating. You probably heard my roar from Melbourne when Jota scored!'

Upon his appointment at Celtic, Postecoglou said he'd been given the honour of leading one of the great names in world football, hailing the club as 'a proper footballing institution and so much more – real history, real substance, real authenticity and real soul'. He may not have grown up listening to tales of the Lisbon Lions or idolising Danny McGrain. He made no attempt to backdate his affection for the club in order to fake a lifelong attachment. But he didn't find it hard to immerse himself in the culture of the club. Or to convince fans that he was the real deal.

As former South Melbourne chairman Nick Galatas, a real football man who has been instrumental in trying to get Australia's most successful ever team back into the big time via the newly formed National Second Tier, puts it: 'People embrace football teams because they love this game, they can't escape it – and they see that passion embodied in Ange. Because he recognises their passion. And because he's immersed in the game.

'The supporters at a massive club like Celtic embraced him because he is *of* the game. He hasn't learned football, he's emerged from it; he's grown up in a proper, passionate, organic football environment. Everything he said was taken to heart by the supporters because they figure: "Hey, this guy gets us." They're right. He does.'

With the benefit of hindsight, the partnership between Postecoglou and Celtic began to look like a near-perfect union. A genuine meeting of hearts and minds. A love story? Sure, why not? Complete with a classic meet cute backstory of a boy, standing in front of a stadium, asking if he can get a tour of the trophy room.

Key Game

ABERDEEN 1 CELTIC 2

Sunday, 3 October 2021

A SCRAPPY victory that kept Celtic sitting in sixth place in the table, behind only Dundee United, Motherwell, Hibs, Hearts and ... well, y'know. A late winner at Pittodrie. A first Scottish Premiership away victory in almost eight long months, stretching back to the dying days of Neil Lennon's second stint as Hoops boss. Significant? You have no idea.

Celtic started this lunchtime match a full six points behind league leaders Rangers, who would beat Hibs at Ibrox later that afternoon. Had Postecoglou's men slipped up here, well, Glasgow Rules dictate that the new manager would have been placed under enormous pressure. From outside critics to sceptical elements within the Celtic support, grumblings would have become full-throated roars of complaint. Maybe even calls for the board to abandon this 'experiment' with a gaffer clearly ill-suited to Scottish football.

To put things in context, Postecoglou's opening months as Celtic boss were every bit as rocky and difficult as he could ever have imagined. And fans, in the main, understood that this was always going to be the case. The new boss inherited a team who had, under Lennon and then interim head coach John Kennedy, failed to win a trophy for the first time since 2010. Those not familiar with Scottish football need to understand how big a deal that is. It's just not acceptable. The Aussie also agreed to take on the gig without bringing in any familiar backroom staff, an absolute rarity in an era when managers insist on contracts for their favourite assistants, analysts, nutritionists and fitness experts. There were, then, extenuating circumstances.

Set against all of that, though, was a set of results that generated genuine fear among supporters who had taken the departure of Brendan Rodgers as hard as any spurned lover, suffered agonies while watching Rangers romp to the 2020–21 title, and who were now being asked to put their faith in a manager whose previous successes in Australia and Japan were viewed, by some, with outright distrust. Knocked out of the Champions League by Midtjylland and beaten 2–1 by Hearts at Tynecastle in their first Premiership fixture of the season, Celtic had rallied to make the Europa League group stages and put together some impressive domestic results, including a pair of 6–0 league wins over Dundee and St Mirren. Heading north to Aberdeen in early October, however, they'd lost the first big derby of the season, courtesy of a Filip Helander header, been beaten by Livingston and only managed to draw with Dundee United. See? He didn't get it. Couldn't adapt to the unique peculiarities of the Scottish game.

Ahead through Kyogo Furuhashi's early opener, Celtic were pegged back by Lewis Ferguson's equaliser early in the second half. Aberdeen then had chances to win the game, with former Hoops captain Scott Brown coming closest with a powerful header saved at point-blank range by Joe Hart. And then Jota, the Portuguese winger with an eye for goal, slid in to finish off a well-executed move to create space for a low cross and a virtual tap-in. Stop us if you've heard that one before.

In the aftermath of the game, Postecoglou spoke not about the skills or footballing smarts demonstrated by his players, but the character they showed to fight back after Aberdeen's equaliser, pointing out: 'That's probably the one thing people were questioning up until now.'

That character, along with improvements in understanding of what the new manager wanted, would rarely be questioned again as Celtic went undefeated, in the Premiership, for the rest of the season. And reclaimed the league flag from their old rivals. Now, that all *might* have happened without Jota's late strike at Pittodrie. In a sport where momentum matters, however, it felt like a turning point at the time. And looks even more important, in retrospect.

Chapter 13

SPURRED ON BY THE DOUBTERS

IF ANGE Postecoglou ever allowed himself to be affected by scepticism among the self-appointed guardians of football's great and inalienable truths, the gatekeepers on a mission to maintain conformity and crush the ambitions of outside agitators, he'd still be standing behind the counter of that bank in Melbourne trying to interest customers in a new savings product. And maybe, just maybe, passing the longest hours by daydreaming about the great coaching career that might have been, if only he'd stuck to his guns.

So, no, it didn't take the foresight of a soothsayer to suggest that he'd be unaffected by a bit of criticism when he got the Tottenham Hotspur gig. Appointed on 6 June 2023 to become the club's fourth manager since the heady heights of reaching the Champions League final in 2019, he was lauded by Spurs chairman Daniel Levy for the attacking style of football he had brought to his previous employers and, in a pointed nod towards the failed experiments that had brought the club to this point, for his track record in developing players. Not to mention, as Levy himself put it, an 'understanding of the importance of the link from the academy'.

Given the travails of previous incumbents, it was never likely to be a walk in the park. Anyone with a modicum of insight into his character could predict that he'd hurl himself headlong into the Premier League with exactly the same single-minded fearlessness that had typified his journey to the promised land of English football. Having waited his whole life for a chance to make a name for himself at one of England's true glamour clubs, he was never going to fail for want of chutzpah. Neither fear of the unknown nor sensitivity to local sentiment was likely to give him so much as a moment's pause.

Regardless of final finish position or points total, Postecoglou was determined that this first season as Spurs manager would be spent reshaping expectations and blowing apart preconceptions about what fans should demand from their team. Pushing the envelope with, at times, an apparent disregard for the scoreboard, the clock or even the league table. Not everyone was an enthusiastic traveller on this leap into the unknown. And every misstep along the way has been hailed as definitive proof, in some quarters, that the Aussie veteran with the laconic demeanour is just another feckless dreamer. Ossie Ardiles with a better stock of one-liners. There are some who will never be convinced.

Any examination of the facts must serve to dispel all but a few lingering doubts. Because the sheer scale of the transformation he has overseen at Tottenham would be impressive in any circumstances. That he did it all while coping with the departure of Harry Kane to Bayern Munich, a loss that would have sent some of his predecessors into a downward spiral of finger-pointing and thinly veiled complaints about 'support' from the board, makes it all the more remarkable. But not really that surprising, when you consider both the man's track record and his ability to hold fast to principles when all around are screaming for an orderly retreat.

From day one at Tottenham, he made himself very clear on exactly what he expected from his players. And what they could expect from him. There would be no half-hearted easing-in period, no striking a balance between soaring ambition and the basic fundamentals held in such reverence by so many in the coaching world. Instead of making his team difficult to beat, he set out to make Spurs everyone's worst nightmare opponent. Relentless, per-petually in motion, forever changing the angles, always bringing a significant element of chaos to the contest. Let the keepers of the game's great secrets carry on preaching about the idiocy of taking unnecessary risks. Nothing they said really mattered to the man at the business end of another footballing revolution.

For those aware of the Ange backstory and the principles that underpin his every decision in football, watching all of this unfold was hugely entertaining. The fun began the moment his name was mentioned in connection with a vacancy in north London. There was enormous comedy value in watching the reaction to Postecoglou's arrival at Spurs. The shocked expressions and statements of disbelief. The bemused mutterings of wise men who could only conclude that the Matrix was glitching. And, of course, the distinctly underwhelming welcome from supporters. Does everyone remember the #NoToAnge social media campaign launched by some Tottenham fans, a direct and distinctly unsubtle response to their club first being linked with

Postecoglou? The tenor of the discourse, in certain corners of an audience convinced that the Aussie represented a step down, seemed to centre around supporters declaring simply: 'We deserve better.' Some of you may have lent your support to those protests, liked a few posts, retweeted a couple of the pithier comments. Maybe even added your own thoughts to the groundswell of anger and disgust over a perceived lowering of expectations when it came to attracting elite coaching talent.

That's okay. Everyone is entitled to their opinion. Generational scar tissue among the Spurs support has to be factored into any argument; they were never going to welcome a left-field appointment and were always likely to listen to the naysayers preaching impending doom. If anyone would have understood this scepticism bordering on disrespect, it would have been Ange himself. He recognised that his appointment was acting as a lightning rod for wider unrest over the running of Tottenham; his recruitment was an easy target for those who saw it as part of a continuing trend. Take a look at the scene he walked into. Kane was on his way out, the all-time club great and occasional messiah having finally lost patience with promises of silverware tomorrow. José Mourinho and Antonio Conte – two picks from the elite end of European coaching talent – had come and gone in quick succession. Nuno Espirito Santo had been . . . well, you know. Many thought the return of Mauricio Pochettino was on the cards. Half a dozen big names were linked with the gig. And now they were appointing this guy? A Celtic manager?

It fitted the easy narrative about a lack of ambition on the part of Daniel Levy, a man hardly renowned for reading the room and acting accordingly. Especially when it was so obvious, to some, that Ange wasn't even his first choice. Call it a perfect storm of unrest and protest. Another reason for the disgruntled to vent their frustrations while fearing the worst. Out there in Pundit Land, of course, there was plenty of manufactured outrage from the usual suspects. How dare Tottenham appoint someone with no experience in a 'major' league? How could they overlook all those candidates with Premier League experience in favour of a guy whose many achievements counted for nothing – less than zero on the show-us-your-medals coefficient table used by English experts – in the grand scheme of modern football? Naturally, there was complete dismissal of everything he'd done in transforming Celtic, with inevitable comments about him moving from a small pond to shark-infested waters. Nice line. Wrong. But pithy.

Former Spurs striker Darren Bent summed up the feelings of many 'experts' when, in the wake of the announcement, he said: 'The fact they have now turned to Postecoglou, you go: "Hmmm, why?" And if you are Postecoglou, knowing they been linked with all these managers, why would you want to go there knowing you are sixth or seventh choice? For me, I just think it is a risk. There would be options I would have ahead of Postecoglou. I'm not trying to diminish anything he's done in Scotland, which is fantastic, but, as we have all seen, the Premier League is a different animal. It's a completely different beast.'

Some went even further, with another ex-Spurs centre forward openly admitting that he was simply 'not familiar' with the new gaffer. Not that it stopped Louis Saha from criticising the decision to appoint the Aussie, saying: 'It's a hard time for Tottenham fans to accept any decision from the club because they are frustrated and have just watched a horrible season, an almost disrespectful season for them with some of the poor results they had. They will comment and criticise Postecoglou's appointment – that's normal – but he does deserve a chance first. Postecoglou will have to prove that he is worthy of being a Premier League and Tottenham's manager. Yes, he's done well with Celtic, but I'm not familiar with him so I'm not surprised some fans are frustrated. Any manager who comes into this role at Tottenham will always be criticised because it's a hard job.'

Even among those willing to give Postecoglou the benefit of the doubt, there was an assumption that he would change his approach, tailoring his tactics to suit an environment unlike anything he'd experienced before. More on that later, but seriously? The first draft of this book was finalised while Ange was still happily building something special in Glasgow. Remarkably, the rewrites required when he took the Spurs job – they began the moment he was mentioned in connection with the gig, obviously – didn't take too long. The furore, the uproar, the dismissive denigrating of his ability, experience and suitability for such a major challenge in the world's greatest league? All of this had happened before. And no-one, least of all the man himself, was going to let the minor details – the abuse, the diminishing of every achievement on his CV, even the absolute certainty that he was far from first choice for the gig – get in the way of his ambition.

Drawing comparisons between his arrival in Scotland and the short hop to the big league over the border,

Postecoglou openly admitted: 'I think in both jobs, no one would say it, but I was last man standing. They ended up being rejected by a fair few and I ended up being the last one left. That's okay, I'll take that. I have to thank Eddie Howe [for the Celtic job]. I think that was pretty much done, and then, for whatever reason, Eddie didn't feel comfortable in taking the role. That had gone so far down the path in pre-season that they had to make a quick decision. I think I was on their list; I had a quick discussion with a couple of the key decision makers, and they saw something in me. I was looking forward to it because it was the bit that had been missing. I'd had success, I knew I could do the job, but I hadn't had it in a place that I knew would be impactful, meaningful. I knew if I had success at Celtic, it would mean something, if only because I knew what it meant to the supporters. If nothing else, I knew I would have an impact in Glasgow.'

Acceptance of how the world works, an understanding that he was never going to be in pole position for the biggest jobs purely because he'd started several thousand miles behind any European rival, is one thing. Anyone watching Ange grin ruefully as he addresses the surprise of supporters, or the outright apathy of commentators entirely immersed in the almighty Premier League, might conclude that he's entirely untroubled by the army of doubters ranged against him at every turn. But that would be wrong.

Remember what long-time assistant Peter Cklamovski told us about his old friend and colleague being driven by pain? Constantly being told that you're not good enough, that nothing you ever do will ever be good enough, has to hurt. So, yeah, even the big man with the gruff demeanour and typically Australian 'no worries' attitude admits to being stung by the same exclusionary arrogance that first prompted him to establish that school team at Prahran High. He'd show 'em.

Postecoglou, the former Socceroos boss who had won the Asian Cup, managed at World Cup and accumulated all manner of honours on the 'wrong' side of Planet Football before finally getting a chance at Celtic, revealed not so long ago that he'd found the entire experience – constantly banging his head against the same brick wall without anyone on the other side even hearing his screams – genuinely 'depressing'. The fact that he didn't just crawl back under his South Melbourne-branded duvet and return to his own corner of the world is surely a source of relief to anyone who has enjoyed watching Spurs or Celtic play with such swagger.

Speaking about how long it took to secure his place on the big stage, Postecoglou said: 'People have only discovered me in the last couple of years, where I have had 25 years of being fairly successful. I didn't understand it, I used to come over here five, six years ago – I was national team boss and people would introduce me to so-and-so. And it was like going to those Hollywood auditions and being rejected – they just didn't know who I was. It was so depressing; I'd been working for 25 years. I never thought I would get here, to be honest, not because of my ability, just because no one was looking this way. People kept telling me: "You are better off being sacked three times in Europe than being successful this side of the world."'

Looking at what Postecoglou achieved at Celtic, and the transformation in style and mood affected during his first season at Tottenham, it's tempting to think that this was always going to happen. That eventually he'd get his break. And make the most of it. Among just a few positive voices making themselves heard amid the cacophony of criticism that greeted his Spurs move, the most optimistic naturally came from someone back home. A compatriot repeatedly linked with – but never hired by – English clubs during a long managerial career. A proud Aussie who felt compelled to stand up for Ange.

Socceroos boss Graham Arnold was nothing if not convincing in his argument in support of the new Tottenham gaffer, declaring: 'I think he'll kill it. He's just totally obsessed with the game. It's his life. I always knew that he had that mentality of where he wanted to go – that was to the top. He had a few setbacks, but that's coaching. You learn from those types of setbacks, and Ange has always been someone that has always been so determined to prove the doubters wrong. That, in a lot of ways, is his motivation. I'm just so happy for him. We've got a hard way for coaching in Australia. One of Ange's hugest strengths is recruitment, and his attention to detail in the players that he gets for his way, the system and the way he wants to play. Because we're coaching with a salary-capped system, we've had to do a lot more work, a lot harder work and focus on the tactical side more than ever. A lot of managers are managers, they're not coaches as well. Ange has the dual role of being a coach as well as a manager. On the tactical side of things, he's not relying on other people to tell him what to do because he's got that nous. On the managerial side, he knows man management, he knows how to get the best out of people and motivate people. Sometimes a lot of managers leave the coaching to someone else to do and they're playing the way of that other coach. With Ange, it's his way. It's fantastic.'

If Arnold's was hardly a lone voice, the strength of his conviction put him in a very small minority. The truth is that, even among those who had marvelled at his mighty works in Japan and Scotland, Postecoglou's move to Spurs felt like a risk. A leap of faith by both parties. In a brutally tough domestic competition, at a club where supporters had been teased and tormented repeatedly, there was bound to be scepticism. But also, because it's the thing that keeps every football fan going back week after sodding week: hope.

Ange managed to quell some of the former, while kindling the latter, simply by being himself. Only more so. A little more self-deprecating, a touch bluffer in his assessment of various crises. Underpinning everything with a very Aussie approach to communication. His handling of the Harry Kane departure, which could easily have become an even bigger soap opera with a more dramatically-inclined gaffer, set the tone for what was to follow. Even if, behind the calm demeanour and 'it is what it is, mate' approach to every question, his heart was going like the clappers at the very thought of kicking off the season without a centre forward almost without equal in world football.

It was only a long time after the fact, towards the end of his first season, that Postecoglou admitted just how difficult it had been when Kane finally joined Bayern Munich just 24 hours before the big kick-off: 'I was literally sitting in here, the day before the Brentford game, and he just left. So you're starting a season and the most significant person at this football club – maybe ever – by the time the dust settles has just left on the eve of the first game. That was going to be a big challenge for us because Harry is the best No. 9 in the world at the moment and he was a consistent goal scorer for this football club in the Premier League. Irrespective of the club's fluctuations, he always scored goals. I remember just making a real conscious effort of the old duck just looking really graceful above the water, and just if there's any panicking happening, just make sure it's under the water where no one can see, particularly the players.'

It probably says something about Postecoglou that, where most people would reach for the more familiar swan analogy to describe the frantic efforts going on just beneath the calm surface, he likened himself to a less flamboyant type of water fowl. He takes matter-of-fact to new levels in conversation or under interrogation, leaving stylistic flourishes to his team. As Spurs fans, be they doubters, shouters or wannabe converts to the Church of Ange, would quickly find out. Starting on match day one of a Premier League adventure guaranteed to generate excitement – and annoy the hell out of everyone who confidently predicted a more pragmatic approach from a man who'd be lucky to get through the first five games without being forced to rethink his bolder-than-bold approach.

Key Game

TOTTENHAM 1 CHELSEA 4

English Premier League
6 November 2023

RIDICULOUS. Genuinely unbelievable to many of those either in attendance or watching at home. How could a team reduced to nine men even contemplate doing . . . that? It's insanity, right? A fixture that requires little in the way of recap, given both the global reach of the Premier League and the cultural crossover appeal of such madcappery run amok, it is worth remembering some of the details from this encounter in north London.

Spurs scored first, very early, through Dejan Kulusevski. Then Christian Romero conceded a penalty, converted by Cole Palmer, with a challenge that saw the Argentine sent off. When Destiny Udoge was also red-carded early in the second half, there could only be one reaction from the Spurs coaching staff, right? Time to sit deeper than a politician's fear of answering a question. Man the barricades and deploy a rolling roadblock no more than 35 yards from goal.

There are two things to note about Postecoglou taking a radically different approach to a problem that would force most tacticians to react as if they were setting up one of those slightly false attack v defence scenarios beloved by UEFA technical department boffins. First? His alternative – possibly the highest defensive line ever deployed by a team reduced to eight outfield players – didn't actually work. Chelsea eventually figured a way to play through a risk-and-reward defence that produced some memorable snapshots, not least one showing a back seven maintaining a strict line no more than two yards inside their own half. It was a failure by Postecoglou, then, to confront reality.

The second point of order? That, although Tottenham's methods might have varied, Ange and his coaching staff were trying to achieve the same goal of any brains trust confronted with a two-man disadvantage. They were trying to reduce the amount of space available to the opposition. Some do it by sitting back. They just did it by forcing a level of syncopated precision, perfect timing between runner and passer, that proved difficult for Chelsea to master. Spurs effectively restricted their opponents to one tactic.

So, while the Tottenham fans who stayed to give their players an uproarious ovation at full-time definitely appreciated Ange's well-practised 'It's just who we are, mate . . .' spiel, there was more to it than just some high-handed desire to put ideological purity ahead of pragmatism. Postecoglou just saw a different potential solution to the problem, based on principles not too dissimilar that would prompt AN Other Coach to signal an ordered retreat from opposition territory.

As for his follow-up statement: 'Even with five men, we'll have a go . . .'? Should IFAB ever get around to rendering such a scenario possible, you wouldn't bet against it.

Chapter 14

A WHOLE NEW BALL GAME

ALL the Ange Postecoglou hallmarks have been there. The refusal to play the scoreboard or the clock. The almost reckless disregard for pragmatism. And a cast-iron belief that this is the only way Tottenham will ever become a truly successful team in a football world skewed by the unlimited riches of sovereign wealth funds. At no point has the Spurs boss even considered taking a backward step. But Postecoglou understands that the only guaranteed way to be overtaken is to stand still. Throughout his career, he has constantly tweaked and adapted his tactics. Like any good coach, he's always looking for the extra 1 per cent that can make all the difference. He's made a life out of finding different ways to dominate opponents, to win and use possession wisely, and to be the better team.

Had Harry Kane stayed at Spurs in the summer of 2023, instead of deciding to chase the promise of more instant success at Bayern Munich, Postecoglou's Tottenham would have played in a slightly different manner, certainly in the final third. And Kane would probably have bagged 30 goals by Easter at the latest. The fact that such an intelligent footballer missed out on working with one of the most astute coaches in the game must go down as a missed opportunity. Together, they would have worked wonders.

Fellow Bayern evacuee Eric Dier's slightly odd insistence that Tottenham did not 'do tactical work' under the new coaching staff, meanwhile, rang far from true to anyone with a basic grasp of Postecoglou's methods. It may not always *seem* like they're working on tactics. But everything, absolutely everything he and his coaches do, from warm-up to activation, passing drill to conditioned games, is about honing the fine details of Angeball. As much as the boss may encourage free thinking and improvisation in the final third, he isn't a guy who leaves much to chance. As he put it: 'We do a lot of work on it. A lot of it is on instincts, but we're trying to create a system, wherever I've been, that is as fluid as it can be.'

The Spurs upgrade on said system has been offensive, bordering on the devil-may-care. But it's also a good deal more structured than it might appear at first glance. The fact that you can't always see the threads linking players and areas of the park is a testament to how well they've weaved the patterns. It all starts, of course, with the build-up. The full backs driving inside to join the holding midfielder, while the centre backs pull wide, isn't just about overloading the central area in case the ball is turned over. This base allows the players ahead of that 2-3 foundation, for want of a better term, to get a little freaky with their movement. No, you won't find those exact words in any UEFA-approved coaching bible. But it rather accurately conveys the rotations, feints, gentle drifts and seismic shifts that the front five – and it is a front five – can use to pull opposition defences out of position, in anticipation of the press being broken. Just copying Pep? Sure. Whatever you say to get a 'like' on your hot take . . .

Postecoglou's Spurs vary how they mess with opponents at the sharp end. Sometimes the front three stay high and pin defenders in place. That allows the playmakers, ideally James Madisson and Pape Sarr when both are fit, to occupy spaces between the lines, drop into receive the ball on the half turn – and then do what comes naturally, knowing that they'll have movement ahead of them and support from behind. On other occasions, you'll see the centre forward – Richarlison, who is most definitely not a typical Ange player – drop off, hoping to drag a defender with him. When that happens, one of the great overlooked tenets of Postecoglou's principles, a willingness to get the ball forward quickly, comes into play. It hasn't been unusual to see possession go straight from goalkeeper to one of the wingers peeling into the gap left by the striker's bit of bump-and-go deception.

None of the work described above is intended to be a reinvention of the 4-3-3. There are plenty of coaches operating at all levels of football who work along similar lines, looking to create numerical or technical overloads, isolating weak links and presenting elite footballers – opponents who can do nine out ten things to a world-class standard – with the one problem guaranteed to make them uncomfortable. Spurs, for all their flaws towards the tail end of Postecoglou's first season at the helm, just happen to be very, very good at it.

The difference between this challenge and all the others faced by Ange over the years, of course, lies in the quality of players available to him – and the class of opposition he's being asked to outsmart. If he will always consider himself fortunate to have worked with some fine footballers earlier in his career, no-one comes close to the ability and athleticism of those he inherited from a series of unsatisfied predecessors. Even allowing for the frenetic pace and relentless competitiveness of the Premier League, having this sort of quality in his armoury has encouraged Postecoglou to push his natural boldness to new extremes. Well, if you had Son Heung-Min in your squad, you'd be tempted to go a little wild too.

Virtually every player in that Spurs squad has the essential skills – not least the sort of all-round vision that makes occupying seemingly unnatural, perhaps even impossible, positions look natural – needed to do what their manager wants. So, as was the case at Celtic, it can be a full back or a central midfielder breaking into the half space, the same entry point Postecoglou's teams have been pounding away at since his first days as a gaffer. It doesn't matter if it's a striker or a winger popping up on the edge of the box. At Spurs, there shouldn't be the variable quality that occasionally caused things to break down at other, lesser clubs. The only problem? Getting them to believe. To truly believe. To commit with everything they've got, regardless of circumstances, to a philosophy that leaves no room for half-heartedness or second guessing. Until and unless Postecoglou has/had a dressing room full of willing converts, Spurs will/would always be limited by their own lack of self-belief. Or, as the manager himself puts it: 'If there's space there, forget that you're a full back; you're a footballer, get in that space. It's up to us to ensure we're covering the gaps that are left. I think once players realise that they have the freedom to do that, it's still very structured, then they don't second guess themselves. They know it doesn't matter if they're a left full back; if there's space there, they get into it.'

Out of possession, well, did anyone expect Ange's Spurs to simply sit off in a low block and let opponents play around them? Pressing, at a time when many in the game are moving away from this most attacking form of defence, has been key at Tottenham. They want the ball. More importantly, they want the other guys not to have the ball. That means going to get it. Which starts from the centre forward angling his press to force play down one side, with support from his wingers and the No. 10. Again, there's nothing particularly revolutionary about trying to trap opponents before they can get out of their own final third, forcing them to play into traffic – or actually generating a turnover by closing off all options, presenting more panicky defenders with plenty of opportunities to flap. But the way Spurs make it work, most of the time, is impressive. The tightness of their discipline should, in theory, reduce the amount of running the midfield three need to do in order to win possession or block passing lanes. Which makes it easier to maintain a seemingly unsustainable tempo for 90 minutes.

Why, then, did they run out of steam when the race for Champions League places required another burst of acceleration late in that first season? What held Tottenham back from carrying that swagger and style all the way through to the end of the campaign? Well, to hear some tell it, the answer is obvious. Postecoglou is a one-trick pony. A busted flush, even. A guy who has been found out now that he's working in a 'proper' league.

Ange himself spoke, towards the end of that first campaign, about the need to believe 'relentlessly' in what he was doing, defending himself from the laziest accusations by pointing out: 'Necessity is the mother of invention. It's probably one of the biggest misconceptions about me, that I've got just one plan. I've used just about every system in the world in my career. Often during games, often during seasons, I've played just about every formation you could care to mention.'

Not everyone was convinced after year one. And there were times, towards the end, when Ange – with his gripes about fragile foundations – seemed almost to lose faith, not necessarily in his methods, but in whether the squad he built for season 2023–24 was strong enough, mentally, to do the necessary. Any doubts were fleeting, however, with friends and confidantes quickly stressing that the manager remained absolutely fixated by a desire – a need, even – to achieve great things with Spurs.

And that invariably means sticking to his guns when it comes to tactics. Even in extremis. Whatever the situation. Because he believes not only that it works, but that it will work brilliantly at Spurs. Not the club with the biggest budget or the most social media followers. But a proper football team, with roots in its community, foundations built on a belief that the beautiful game should be played in a certain way – and that all of this should be possible while winning trophies. When he took the job, it was tempting for many to suggest that Postecoglou had jumped at the first big Premier League offer dangled in front of him. There's some truth in that. But he chose Spurs. He willingly walked into a club that had driven proven managers like

Mourinho, Pochettino and Conte to the brink and beyond.

Speaking much later about why he decided to turn Tottenham immediately into an all-attack team rather than gently bleeding his ideas into established patterns of play, he said simply: 'I felt the club was ready for that. They were seeking a change. There was no point appointing me otherwise. In the discussions we had, I told them this is what I was going to do, and I wasn't going to compromise. It's going to be scary, not always smooth. I think there was a willingness from the club; I think that is the space they are most comfortable with, and that suits me. It is challenging, but I love that. It's easy for me to talk about these things, that we're going to play out from the back, be expansive. It leaves you vulnerable. All I could tell the players was: "If it doesn't work, it's on me. Don't play with any fear – go and play." I've really enjoyed how they have embraced that. It hasn't been tested yet, and it will get tested, we will have stumbles along the way for sure, but I'm really pleased how they have taken on the way we are going to play. It can't just be a desperation for just a trophy. This club is more than that. I don't see this as a club where just a trophy is enough. I know why there's such a desperation because there has been such a long drought, but it is not what I want to build. I want to build a club where every year we are fighting for trophies.'

It's important to remember that. During the breakthrough first season, Postecoglou would certainly have liked some silverware. Even if his refusal to go all-in when competing in the League Cup left plenty of supporters feeling far from satisfied. At a club where the damage done by short-termism should be clear to everyone, he wanted to lay the foundations for something lasting. And, yes, to be responsible for the creation of a footballing model that cannot be measured in medals alone.

In that first season, the technical satisfaction of seeing Plans A, B and C work – to varying degrees – was completely outweighed by contentment of being responsible for the regular generation of widespread emotional uproar. Especially at home. The last-minute winners and dramatic fightbacks, the raucous joy of being right at the heart of the party when supporters go completely unhinged with delight/disbelief/relief as their team – very much their team again, in so many important ways – do something utterly remarkable . . . all of that is as precious as gold to the little kid from Prahran who grew up to love this game to the point of obsession.

In a moment of quiet reflection on strides taken and missteps committed during that debut campaign, Postecoglou talked warmly about his players repaying supporters by producing memories that will live forever. The comebacks – take your pick from a handful of victories, or maybe even the 3-3 draw away to Man City, for obvious reasons – and celebrations that made the world seem like a much fairer place from a Spurs perspective. The passing connections and exhilarating attacks that make you know, in your marrow, that you're watching something special. That's what matters most.

Because we have to go back, always, to Ange's founding motivation. The lessons learned at the feet of his father, honed as a captain under the legendary Ferenc Puskás, perfected through trial by fire as a coach from the wrong side of the world, preaching ideas running so contrary to established thinking that he was dismissed as a dangerous radical. All of the hurt and frustration, each instance of hope and elation, helps explain why he summed up his first season of education in the Premier League by saying: 'The supporters here are going to get some heroes to follow. And that's what they want – players they can worship.'

Chapter 15

ANGEBALL 2.0, 3.0 ... AND BEYOND

ANGE Postecoglou is building a Tottenham team capable, he hopes, of winning the Premier League. And the Champions League? Sure. Why not? Having waited half a century to be called home to his own footballing mothership, the country whose game he devoured as a kid growing up in 1970s Australia, he was never going to go at this half-hearted.

Football's approach to long-term strategic thinking tends to be on a par with the average dieter's commitment to lasting lifestyle changes. It all makes so much sense. But sticking to the plan when you can't see immediate results and morale is crashing faster than your blood sugar? Temptation thrives in that sweet spot of uncertainty. And Tottenham are, historically, particularly ill-equipped to resist the inevitable urge to start all over (again). Every time someone asks about the next move in Ange Postecoglou's footballing journey, then, it's important to remember that he's never further than a handful of missteps away from getting the boot. That's just how the game works.

Assuming no catastrophic collapse in the immediate future, however, the ultimate destination for this Aussie adventurer should not be in any doubt. Titles and cups, of course. And, having taken on an impossible challenge in guiding Celtic into Champions League combat against the mighty Real Madrid, Postecoglou burns with a desire – a need, even – to take a more ready and capable team into UEFA's flagship competition. While he would never have sacrificed building solid foundations for the short-term high of finishing fourth in the Premier League in his first season at Spurs, returning to the elite end of European football is a priority. A necessity.

Socceroos legend Paul Wade summed up the general feeling among those with a decent bead on Ange's intentions when he said: 'It feels like he belongs in the Champions League. No doubt about it. He was winning things in Melbourne, then he went to Brisbane and educated the whole country with Roarcelona, playing out from the back. People were like: "Hold on, we've never seen anything like this." He changed the mindset about how we play football, the style of football we play in Australia. It all started with him. When you go to another country, like Japan, it can be tough. Yes, they're really respectful. But he didn't speak the language and he got a group of players who he won over right away. So he can do anything. Absolutely anything.'

Celtic won a fair number of plaudits for their Champions League performances, not least for having a proper Ange-style go at Real in the Santiago Bernabéu, in season 2022–23. But they finished bottom of a group that also included RB Leipzig and Shakhtar Donetsk, conceding 15 goals and scoring just four in reply. A pair of draws against the Ukrainians was as good as it got, in terms of results. Postecoglou, roundly criticised by some for not adapting his tactics to the challenge, repeatedly insisted that the only way his team could ever progress, could ever grow into a side capable of going further in Europe, was by sticking to a style designed to outplay opponents.

For many of his old friends and colleagues, of course, there was a basic thrill in seeing Postecoglou standing on the touchline in Madrid, or listening to Celtic Park reverberate to the strains of 'You'll Never Walk Alone' on one of those enormous Champions League nights in the east end of Glasgow – still one of the great occasions in the whole European football experience. Lifelong Celtic fan Steve Blair smiled as he addressed the once-impossible incongruity of seeing his former team-mate grace the most well-dressed stage in club football, the big man leaning back in his chair at one of our enjoyable meetings in Melbourne and recalling: 'I remember me and him training, breaking up into twos. It was always us because we were mates and defenders. Just doing stupid drills. Only half an hour from here . . . the main ground didn't have floodlights and the training ground had a pole with one little light we had to train around. It was half dark and half light. We used to finish up with a wee small-sided game. We had to move the goals, so they were in the light. So, when I think of us from there to him leading Celtic out in the Bernabéu Stadium or him leading Celtic out in a cup final at Hampden . . . from here to there, it's just absolutely amazing. It's a story worth telling.'

Postecoglou's own take on the transformation job to be done at Tottenham, of course, is based on a belief that he can turn Spurs into the best team in Europe. And prove it by dominating all other challengers. If that seemed like a long way off at the end of his first season in North London, well, he expected as much. And was occasionally called upon to recalibrate the expectations of supporters at a club struggling to close ground on their local rivals. A team which lost its record-breaking goal-scoring talisman on the eve of the new campaign. Without wishing to kill the romantic sense of optimism that made the Spurs job so attractive in the first place, he constantly had to explain himself.

During one of the 2023–24 wobbles, it was a pleasure to accept an invitation back onto the Last Word on Spurs podcast. The lads were seeking reassurances, from someone who had done the homework on Ange, that it wasn't all going to fall apart. That it wasn't going to go completely Spurs-y, in other words. During our conversation on Postecoglou's avowed aversion to pragmatism, it was suggested that he couldn't possibly be satisfied with just chasing a Champions League place and reaching the odd cup final. Having won league titles in Australia, Japan and Scotland, he would settle for nothing less in England. A matter of three weeks later, the man himself started saying the same things. In a more eloquent manner, of course. But the messaging was identical.

So, for the benefit of those who didn't heed the warnings of all the former colleagues, players, chairmen and observers who lined up to contribute to the first edition of this book, before Postecoglou swapped Celtic Park for North London, a reminder. This is what he does. This is how he does it. How he's approached football since that first interim head coaching position at South Melbourne. The fact that he's now operating in the Premier League, no longer quite as competitive as it once was from the very pinnacle to the depths of the relegation zone but still a brutally tough division capable of punching holes in the best-laid plans of many a clever gaffer, was never going to force this veteran of Australian, Greek, Japanese and Scottish club football, not to mention his international experience, to take a backward step.

Why? Because he was never making decisions based on a plan to secure fourth place in his first season at Spurs. Such short-termism is anathema to a man who genuinely believes himself capable of winning the very biggest prizes in football, if he gets the right support. After the season was finished, with Tottenham in fifth spot and everyone searching around for a pigeonhole that would fit in their end-of-year wraps and deep dives into winners and losers, Ange felt compelled to point out: 'I never said I didn't care about finishing top four. What I said was that finishing top four does not mean we're going to be the team I want us to be next year. That's not what will define us. Finishing fourth and getting into the Champions League doesn't make you a Champions League club. To be at that level requires more than finishing fourth one year. Do I believe right now we're a Champions League club? No, we're not. We've still got work to do. That doesn't mean I don't want us to reach the Champions League.'

Why does European progress matter, as a measure of external validation? Well, as Postecoglou understands, there is an international exchange rate when it comes to placing a value on trophies won, undefeated runs compiled, or bold strategic strokes pulled off in this or that competition. The Yokohama players who railed against him during his early days in Japan were motivated, in part, by their low opinion of everything he'd achieved in Australia. On the grounds that, well, it was Australia. The same snobbery was at work, twice over, among Celtic fans who doubted that the Postecoglou process – successful in the A-League, perfectly adequate for building a winning team in Japan – could translate to the frenzied mayhem of Scottish football.

So, Spurs supporters using every available platform to cite the pursuit of Postecoglou as further evidence of the bin fire raging out of control at their club? That was entirely inevitable, even before the failures – in quick succession – of Steven Gerrard at Aston Villa and Brendan Rodgers at Leicester City further devalued his achievements as Celtic manager. By any criteria, he was an oddity among a list of big-name candidates more in keeping with the glamour of a club that has always carried itself with a certain panache.

Anyone with a deeper understanding of Postecoglou's career path, however, would understand why Daniel Levy made such a bold/brave/foolhardy move. Whatever your views on Scottish football's suitability for producing either players or coaches, the sustained excellence of Celtic over the course of season 2022–23 – a treble-winning campaign – felt like a major leap in evolution. A sort of iOS update on a footballing model containing just a few minor bugs. Angeball 2.0, even.

To the faithful who call Celtic Park Paradise, of course, the games they watched represented something more significant than a mere upgrade. Among this particular congregation, the football played between kicking off on 31 July 2022 and Callum McGregor lifting the Scottish Cup aloft at Hampden on 3 June 2023 represented an expression of faith. A testament to the power of believing in a purpose beyond just winning. Which is why his leaving hit so many so hard. It is also true to say that the entertainment provided over those ten months – a run of competitive fixtures notable not merely for the trophies lifted, but the near-total domination of Celtic's putative rivals across the city – represented the culmination of more than just a couple of years' work. Here was proof of the theorems Postecoglou had been studying since childhood. A living, breathing, all-powerful illustration of the concepts that, for most of his coaching career, have held the key not merely to victory, but to total control of games.

In Australia, Japan, Scotland and now the world's most competitive league, he has shown that his methods are transferrable, his style of play substantial enough to conquer all sorts of opponents in wildly different environments. And he's demonstrated an ability to turn a team around, to come through initial difficulties and chart a new path to higher ground, that was always going to make him a sought-after talent in a fickle managerial market.

The importance of Celtic kicking on in year two of Postecoglou's reign should not be understated, in this respect. In an age when coaching staffs tend not to hang around for long stints building lasting projects, there was a definite value in the manager – and his players – improving in all departments. No one-season wonders, Celtic established themselves as the undisputed best team in Scotland. Yeah, okay, readers south of the Border can hold the punchlines. It's not as easy as it looks. Why did it matter so much, this continuation of upward trends? After all, the 32-game unbeaten run Celtic put together in clinching the 2021–22 Premiership title was already setting the bar high. Well, according to Postecoglou's view of football, the game most definitely has its equivalent of music's tricky second album. Never more comfortable than during the difficult early days in a job, when all around are doubting him and calls to abandon his 'suicidal tactics' are being shouted from every corner, he admits to suffering – ever so slightly – from greater doubts when the critics have been shut up by win after win. It's a version of what some psychologists call paradise syndrome. Standing on top of the mountain, where else is there to go, right?

To put it in his own words: 'The hardest part, once you've had success, is: "What's the next layer?" That's the most challenging time for me. I question myself when things are going well. What's the next step, the next evolution in what we're doing?' Squeezing the life out of opponents and generating unforced errors by the dozen, Celtic stormed to a second consecutive Scottish Premiership title at a pace that cost one Rangers manager his job – and left another belatedly admitting to a sizeable gulf between Scotland's No. 1 team and their nominal challengers. There weren't many among the Light Blue legions who could deny the obvious, with the massive gap between the sides in the final league table telling only half the story.

What might he have done with Celtic in the Champions League had he not been lured south to take on one of the glamour jobs in English football? We'll never know. It's a fact of footballing life in Glasgow, of course, that anyone achieving that success will not hang around very long. The narrative surrounding Postecoglou, and particularly his next move in the game, was established from the moment he won that first title. By the time he added a second, partly because Rangers' challenge wasn't strong enough to make a good storyline for more than a day or two, everyone had an opinion on whether Ange would be tempted away by the right sort of Premier League offer – or stay around to take another crack at Europe.

Among his close confidantes, there was always an understanding that their old pal had ambitions beyond Celtic Park. His track record shows that, when the time is right, he'll make the decision that suits him best. Is even the most naïve of badge-kissing punters surprised by this? It's a business. Tottenham felt like the perfect next chapter. And everyone loves a good story.

Postecoglou's own personal tale of overcoming adversity, starting with being raised in a country where football was a semi-professional minority sport, was always guaranteed to grab the attention. And it's not over yet. Spend any time speaking to the people who know Ange and they'll tell you how insatiable he is when it comes to acquiring and updating knowledge, as he looks to stay relevant to the next generation. Always learning about football, he makes a genuine effort to find the triggers that will work for a player born in the early 2000s; they're not always the same buttons that would have prompted a 20-something Postecoglou to respond in training or a game. By his own admission, he'll know it's time to walk away from the game when he can no longer hold the attention of a dressing room. When he feels the message isn't getting through.

So far, in all manner of situations and settings, he's been able to keep his messaging up to date. Finding different ways to tell a very personal story with a wider resonance. Postecoglou possibly summed up his belief system best of all in a March 2020 interview with Anthony Hudson of the Masterminds High Performance Sports podcast, saying: 'I grew up in a country where football was a semi-pro game with not a lot of opportunities. All these years later, I've coached at a World Cup, I've won titles, I've done things that are remarkable because I believed in something that was an unknown for an Australian. I feel overwhelmingly blessed with the experiences I've had. Because of that, I can tell that story. I want to do things that are different, I want to do things that stand out, I want people to talk about my teams beyond just the success they have.

'I always say to young coaches that if you want to know what your philosophy is, I can do it for you in one exercise. Imagine there was a game this weekend that was going to decide whether you have a coaching career or not. How would you play? That's your coaching philosophy. If your natural inclination is to say: "You know what? If it's that big a game, if it's that important, we're going to set up to be hard to beat, we don't lose goals, we don't take risks . . ." That's your journey. Take it and make it what you want. If there was a game this weekend that would decide if I had a coaching career or not, I would go for it – and want as many goals as possible.

'So, with every beginning, I try to tell players a story. Everything remarkable that has ever been achieved in this world has begun with people not believing it can be done. When I begin the story, I tell them that what we're going to embark on now is going to be looked upon with sceptical eyes, there will be a lot of pessimism and misunderstanding of what we're trying to do. But that's how you achieve remarkable things in life. We know what is known in the world, what has already been achieved. It's about what we can do that's unknown. You have to take risks, have to believe in something that's sometimes not tangible. By telling that story in chapters, where I'm always predicting the next step for them, players, staff and clubs buy into it more and more. In many respects, I'm telling my story, telling my father's story. When it comes from something as deep as that, the players understand I'm not just spinning something to give them a message; it's a journey I've lived.'